Editor
Mary S. Jones, M.A.

Managing Editor
Karen J. Goldfluss, M.S. Ed.

Cover Artist
Brenda DiAntonis

Art Production Manager
Kevin Barnes

Art Coordinator
Renée Christine Yates

Imaging
Rosa C. See

Publisher
Mary D. Smith, M.S. Ed.

DAILY WARM-UPS

Math

GRADE 6

- Over 300 daily math warm-ups
- Includes practice in five key areas:
  - Numbers and Numeration
  - Operations
  - Measurement and Geometry
  - Graphs, Data, and Probability
  - Algebra, Patterns, and Functions
- Ideal for review and test preparation!

D1450678

Beling

Author

Heath Roddy

Teacher Created Resources, Inc.
6421 Industry Way
Westminster, CA 92683
www.teachercreated.com
ISBN: 978-1-4206-3964-3
©2006 Teacher Created Resources, Inc.
Reprinted, 2009
Made in U.S.A.

Table of Contents

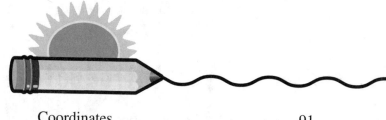

Table of Contents

Introduction

The *Daily Warm-Ups: Math* series was written to provide students with frequent opportunities to master and retain important math skills. The unique format used in this series provides students with the opportunity to improve their own fluency in math. Each section consists of at least 30 pages of challenging problems that meet national and state standards. (See Table of Contents to find a listing of specific subject areas. Answer keys are located at the back of each section.) Use the tracking sheet on page 6 to record which warm-up exercises you have given to your students. Or, distribute copies of the sheet for students to keep their own record.

This book is divided into five sections. The sections are as follows:

- Numbers and Numeration
- Operations
- Measurement and Geometry
- Graphs, Data and Probability
- Algebra, Patterns and Functions

Daily Warm-Ups: Math gives students a year-long collection of challenging problems to reinforce key math skills taught in the classroom. As students become active learners in discovering mathematical relationships, they acquire a necessary understanding that improves their problem-solving skills and, therefore, boosts their confidence in math. When using this book, keep the idea of incorporating the warm-ups with the actual curriculum that you may be currently using in your classroom. This provides students with a greater chance of mastering the math skills.

This book can be used in a variety of ways. However, the exercises in this book were designed to be used as warm-ups where students will have the opportunity to work problems and obtain immediate feedback from their teacher. To help ensure student success, spend a few moments each day discussing problems and solutions. This extra time will not take very long and will yield great results from students! As you use this book, you will be excited to watch your students discover how exciting math concepts can be!

Teaching Tips

Ideas on how to use the warm-ups are as follows:

- *Discussion*—Most warm-ups can be completed in a short amount of time. When time is up, model how to correctly work the problems. You may wish to have students correct their own work. Allow time for students to discuss problems and their solutions to problems. You may want to allow students the opportunity to discuss their answers or the way they solved the problems with partners. Discuss why some answers are correct and why others are not. Students should be able to support their choices. Having students understand that there are many ways of approaching a problem and strategies used in dealing with them are a great benefit for all students. The time you allow students to do this is just as important as the time spent completing the problems.

- *Review*—Give students the warm-up at the end of the lesson as a means of tying in an objective taught that day. The problems students encounter on each warm-up are designed to improve math fluency and are not intended to be included as a math grade. If the student has difficulty with an objective, review the material again with him or her independently and provide additional instruction.

Teaching Tips (cont.)

- *Assessment*—The warm-ups can be used as a preliminary assessment to find out what your students know. Use the assessment to tailor your lessons.

- *Introduction*—Use the warm-ups as an introduction into the new objective to be taught. Select warm-ups according to the specific skill or skills to be introduced. The warm-ups do not have to be distributed in any particular order.

- *Independent Work*—Photocopy the warm-up for students to work on independently.

- *Transparencies*—Make overhead transparencies for each lesson. Present each lesson as a means of introducing an objective not previously taught, or have students work off the transparency.

- *Model*—Invite students to come to the board to model how they approached a problem on the warm-up.

- *Test Preparation*—The warm-ups can be a great way to prepare for math tests in the classroom or for any standardized testing. You may wish to select warm-ups from all sections to use as practice tests and/or review prior to standardized testing.

Student Tips

Below is a chart that you may photocopy and cut out for each student. It will give students a variety of strategies to use when dealing with difficult problems.

✂- -

Math Tips

✓ Write word problems as number problems.

✓ Underline the question and circle any key words.

✓ Make educated guesses when you encounter multiple-choice problems or problems with which you are not familiar.

✓ Leave harder problems for last. Then, come back to solve those problems after you have completed all other problems on the warm-up.

✓ Use items or problem-solving strategies, such as drawing a diagram or making a table to solve the problem.

✓ Always check your answer to see that it makes sense.

Numbers and Numeration Warm-Ups

1	✓	8		15		22		29		36		43		50		57	
2		9		16		23		30		37		44		51		58	
3		10		17		24		31		38		45		52		59	
4		11		18		25		32		39		46		53		60	
5		12		19		26		33		40		47		54		61	
6		13		20		27		34		41		48		55		62	
7		14		21		28		35		42		49		56			

Operations Warm-Ups

1		8		15		22		29		36		43		50		57	
2		9		16		23		30		37		44		51		58	
3		10		17		24		31		38		45		52		59	
4		11		18		25		32		39		46		53		60	
5		12		19		26		33		40		47		54		61	
6		13		20		27		34		41		48		55		62	
7		14		21		28		35		42		49		56			

Measurement and Geometry Warm-Ups

1		8		15		22		29		36		43		50		57	
2		9		16		23		30		37		44		51		58	
3		10		17		24		31		38		45		52		59	
4		11		18		25		32		39		46		53		60	
5		12		19		26		33		40		47		54		61	
6		13		20		27		34		41		48		55		62	
7		14		21		28		35		42		49		56			

Graphs, Data and Probability Warm-Ups

1		8		15		22		29		36		43		50		57	
2		9		16		23		30		37		44		51		58	
3		10		17		24		31		38		45		52		59	
4		11		18		25		32		39		46		53		60	
5		12		19		26		33		40		47		54		61	
6		13		20		27		34		41		48		55		62	
7		14		21		28		35		42		49		56			

Algebra, Patterns and Functions Warm-Ups

1		8		15		22		29		36		43		50		57	
2		9		16		23		30		37		44		51		58	
3		10		17		24		31		38		45		52		59	
4		11		18		25		32		39		46		53		60	
5		12		19		26		33		40		47		54		61	
6		13		20		27		34		41		48		55		62	
7		14		21		28		35		42		49		56			

NUMBERS AND NUMERATION

DAILY Warm-Up 1

Name Belina **Date** _____

1. In Mr. Kingman's math class, $\frac{4}{5}$ of the students earned an "A" on their math exam. The rest of the class earned a "B". What percent of the class earned an "A"? What percent of the class earned a "B"? (*Show your work and circle your final answer.*)

$$100 \div 5 = 20 \qquad 20 \times 4 = 80 \qquad 1 - \boxed{80\%}$$
$$2 - \boxed{20\%}$$

2. At a fishing contest, $\frac{3}{5}$ of the fish caught by the men had a length of 18 inches or longer. Altogether, there were 45 fish caught in the tournament. How many of the fish caught were 18 inches or longer in length? (*Show your work and circle your final answer.*)

$$45 \div 5 = 7 \qquad 7 \times 3 = 21 \qquad 1 - \boxed{21}$$

DAILY Warm-Up 2

Name Bina **Date** B3

1. Use comparative symbols in the problems below.

A. $\frac{3}{4}$ $\bigcirc$ > 0.71   **B.** $\frac{2}{5}$ $\bigcirc$ < 0.40   **C.** $\frac{2}{3}$ $\bigcirc$ < 0.68

2. There are 120 members on the Wharton football team. Of those members, 10% will not take part in Friday's football game due to illness. What should you do to find how many members of the team will be taking part in the game?

Explain: Find out what 10% of 120 is. Subtract that from 120. That is how many players are participating.

 **DAILY** Warm-Up 3 Name **Belina** Date _____

1. Circle the number below that is **not** a common multiple of 4 and 8.

16   24   (28)   32   48

2. Which is a correct definition of an **integer**? (*Circle the correct letter.*)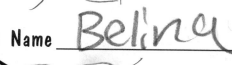

A. An integer includes only whole numbers.

B. An integer includes whole numbers, negative whole numbers, and zero.

C. An integer includes only positive numbers.

D. none of the above

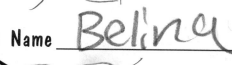 **DAILY** Warm-Up 4 Name **Belina** Date _____

1. Yolanda has a small picture frame she wants to put gold lace around. She bought 1 foot of lace for the frame. She used $8\frac{3}{4}$ inches of lace on the frame. How much lace does Yolanda have left? (*Show your work and circle your final answer.*)

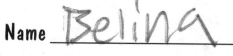

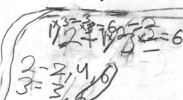

$3/6 + 2/6 = (5/6)$

2. Brandi and Gordon sold raffle tickets for their church group. Of the tickets sold, Brandi sold $\frac{1}{3}$ of the tickets and Gordon sold $\frac{1}{2}$ of the tickets. Their mother asked them, "What fraction of the tickets sold did you sell altogether?" What correct response did Brandi and Gordon give? (*Show your work and circle your final answer.*)

Name Belina

Date _____

Warm-Up 5

1. Which answer choice best describes an **exponent?** (*Circle the correct letter.*)

   A. It is a number with 2 factors.

   B. It is a number with 2 or more factors.

   C. It is a number that is to be multiplied by the base number.

   D. It is a common factor to both numbers involved.

2. Create a factor tree showing the prime factorization for the number 72. Write and circle your final answer using exponents.

72

Name _____ name don't **Date** _____

Warm-Up 6

1. Circle the greater of the two fractions below. How can you tell that it's greater?

$$\frac{4}{16} < \frac{4}{8}$$

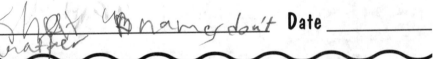

Explain: $\frac{4}{8} > \frac{4}{16}$ so $\frac{4}{8} > \frac{4}{16}$ _____

_____

_____

2. Shade the model to show the mixed number $3\frac{5}{6}$.

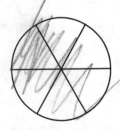 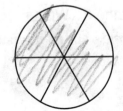  

Name _____ **Date** _____

Warm-Up 7

1. Look at the number below. What prime factorization is the number showing? (*Circle the correct letter.*)

   A. 30   **C.** 50

   B. 40   **D.** 60

   $$5 \times 3 \times 2^2$$

2. David owns a large rectangular lot behind his house. On Saturday morning, he mowed $\frac{1}{4}$ of the lot. That afternoon, he mowed $\frac{3}{8}$ of the lot. He planned to mow the rest on Sunday. Which model can be used to represent the amount of the lot David has already mowed? (*Circle the correct letter.*)

   A.

   C.

   B.

   D.

Name _____ **Date** _____

Warm-Up 8

1. Robert has a collection of wooden blocks. The table shows the color and number he has of each block. Which color blocks does Robert have the most of? (*Circle the correct letter.*)

   A. Yellow   **C.** Red

   B. Black   **D.** Orange

Color	Number	
Yellow	$\frac{2}{3}$	
Black	$\frac{1}{4}$	
Red	$\frac{5}{6}$	
Orange	$\frac{7}{12}$	

2. Look at the tally sheet. It shows the number of votes cast for different students running for class president. How is the fraction of votes Sue received written as a decimal? (*Circle the correct letter.*)

   A. 4.0   **C.** 0.4

   B. 0.04   **D.** 4.04

Students	Votes
Betty	⦀⦀ ⦀⦀ ⦀⦀⦀⦀
Sue	⦀⦀ ⦀⦀ ⦀⦀ ⦀⦀
Marie	⦀⦀ ⦀⦀ ⦀
Vivian	⦀⦀

Name NveBelina **Date** _____

1. Out of the 25 families Mark delivered newspapers to on Sunday, 10 families were home and the rest were away. How is the fraction of newspapers delivered to families not home written as a decimal? (*Show your work and circle your final answer.*)

$10-25 = 15 \frac{3}{5} = 0.60$

2. Salvador bought a 7-foot rope to tie his boat to the dock when he goes fishing. The rope is too long, so Salvador cuts exactly $2\frac{3}{4}$ feet off the rope. How long is Salvador's rope now? (*Show your work and circle your final answer.*)

$7ft - 2\frac{3}{4}ft = 4\frac{1}{4}ft.$

Name Adele **Date** 9/24/19

1. Michael is playing a factors game in math class. The object of the game is to find a match to the factor he draws from the deck. The card below is the one Michael drew. Which card will Michael need to draw to find a match? (*Circle the correct letter.*)

$$6^3 \times 9^4$$

A. 6 x 6 x 6 x 9 x 9 x 9 x 9

C. 6 x 6 x 6 x 6 x 9 x 9

B. 6 x 6 x 9 x 9 x 9 x 9 x 9

D. 6 x 6 x 6 x 6 x 9 x 9

2. What is another way to write 3 x 3 x 3 x 6 x 6? (*Circle the correct letter.*)

A. $6^3 \times 3^3$ **B.** $3^3 \times 6^3$ **C.** $3^3 \times 6^2$ **D.** $3^3 \times 2^6$

Name Belina **Date** _____

1. Which is **true** about composite numbers? (*Circle the correct letter.*)

A. Composite numbers have only one factor.

B. Composite numbers have only two factors.

C. Composite numbers have two or more factors.

D. Composite numbers are only odd numbers.

2. Which answer shows the prime factorization for the number 36? (*Circle the correct letter.*)

A. 2 x 2 x 2 x 2 x 3

B. 3 x 3 x 2 x 2

C. 2 x 2 x 2 x 3 x 3

D. 2 x 2 x 3 x 3 x 3

Name Adele **Date** 9/26/19

1. Jennifer and Megan are making decorations for the school dance. In the time it takes Jennifer to make 4 decorations, Megan makes 1 decoration. By the end of the day, Megan makes 167 decorations. How many decorations did Jennifer make? (*Show your work and circle your final answer.*)

668 decorations

167
x   4
448

2. Roger is planting flowers down the side of his house. He can plant 3 flowers every 2 minutes. If Roger continues to plant the flowers at the same rate, how many flowers will Roger plant in 30 minutes? (*Show your work and circle your final answer.*)

45

DAILY Warm-Up 13

Name **Adele** Date **10/3/19**

1. Elizabeth is having her birthday party. Her mom filled a fraction of the glasses with punch. Which answer below shows an **equivalent fraction** of the glasses Elizabeth's mom filled? (*Circle the correct letter.*)

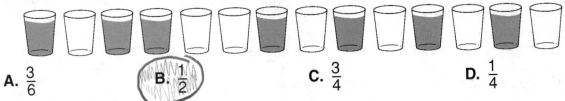

A. $\frac{3}{6}$ B. $\frac{1}{2}$ (circled)   C. $\frac{3}{4}$ D. $\frac{1}{4}$

½
3,5

2. Look at the models below. The first model shows the fraction $\frac{3}{4}$. Shade in an **equivalent fraction** on the second model. What fraction did you shade?

3,14|15

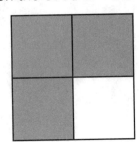 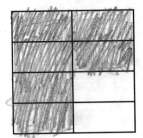 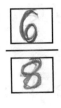

$\frac{6}{8}$

- -

DAILY Warm-Up 14

Name **Adele** Date **10/3/19**

1. List the fractions below in order from least to greatest.

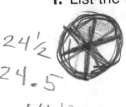

$\frac{1}{2}$ $\frac{1}{4}$ $\frac{2}{3}$ $\frac{3}{4}$ $\frac{2}{6}$

24½
24.5

Least →

1	2	1	2	3
4	6	2	3	4

$\frac{4}{10}$
$\frac{48}{100}$

2. Jackie is on the swim team. She swam the 40-meter dash in 24.488 seconds. What is this number rounded to the nearest tenth?

100   10   1   ¹/₁₀   ¹/₁₀₀   ¹/₁₀₀₀

24.5

1. Ellia and Cody are playing a math game. When Ellia lays down her fraction cards, Cody must lay down decimal cards that show the correct decimal equivalents for the fractions. If Cody did this correctly, which sequence below shows the correct order of the decimals in relation to the fraction cards? (*Circle the correct letter.*)

   A. 2.5, 0.75, 0.25, 0.20

   B. 2.5, 0.75, 0.20, 0.25

   C. 0.20, 0.25, 0.75, 2.5

   D. 0.20, 0.25, 2.5, 0.75

   | $\frac{1}{5}$ | $\frac{1}{4}$ | $\frac{3}{4}$ | $\frac{5}{2}$ |

2. Jamison has 5 green hair ribbons and 6 blue hair ribbons in a box on her dresser. What is the ratio of the number of blue hair ribbons to the total number of green and blue hair ribbons?

---

1. The problem below is one that Lee wrote on the board. Which answer choice solves Lee's problem? (*Circle the correct letter.*)

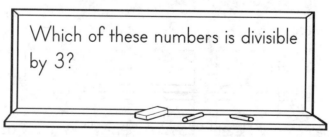

Which of these numbers is divisible by 3?

   A. 1,587,039   **B.** 2,392,643   **C.** 3,968,933   **D.** 5,998,777

2. If each square represents 1 inch on each side, what is the area of the shaded region?

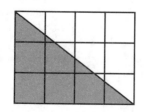

The area of the shaded region is _____ square inches.

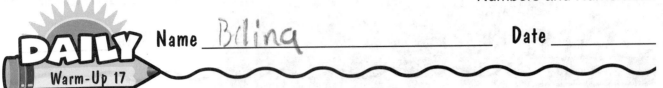

DAILY
Warm-Up 17

1. Position the following set of integers correctly on the number line below.

+8   -2   +2   +12   -9

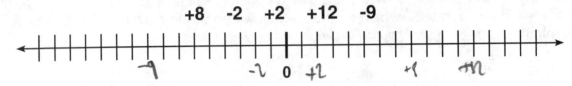

Explain which integer is greater: -2 or +2? _____+2_____

_____

2. Henry and Deron are playing a card game. Of the 24 cards with which each player began the game, Henry has $\frac{1}{2}$ of his cards left and Deron has $\frac{1}{8}$ remaining. How many total cards does each player have?

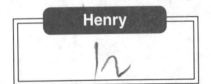

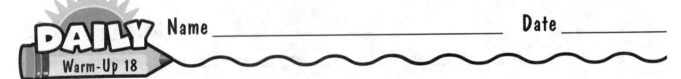

DAILY
Warm-Up 18

1. What factors represent $8^4 \times 9^6$? (*Circle the correct letter.*)

A. 8 x 8 x 8 x 8 x 9 x 9 x 9 x 9 x 9 x 9 x 9

B. 8 x 8 x 8 x 8 x 8 x 8 x 9 x 9 x 9 x 9

C. 8 x 8 x 8 x 8 x 9 x 9 x 9 x 9 x 9 x 9

D. 8 x 8 x 8 x 9 x 9 x 9 x 9

2. Curtis has 80 baseball cards. He sold 75% of them. How many baseball cards did Curtis sell? (*Show your work and circle your final answer.*)

Name _____ **Date** _____

Warm-Up 19

1. Robin is counting the cars parked in a large parking lot and finds that there are exactly 120 cars. She starts counting again and notices that 40 of the first 60 cars are blue. If the color of cars parked in the lot continues at this rate, how many cars parked in the lot will be blue? (*Show your work and circle your final answer.*)

2. Pete, Mary, and Lou are trying to find out whose pencil is the shortest. Pete's pencil is 3.45 inches long. Mary's pencil is 3.87 inches long. Lou's pencil is between the length of Pete and Mary's pencil lengths. Which could be the length of Lou's pencil? (*Circle the correct letter.*)

   A. 3.45 in.　　**B.** 3.78 in.　　**C.** 3.98 in.　　**D.** 2.48 in.

Name _____ **Date** _____

Warm-Up 20

1. Frank and his brother ordered a pizza. Frank ate $\frac{9}{16}$ of the pizza and his brother ate $\frac{2}{16}$ of the pizza. How much more pizza did Frank eat than his brother did? (*Circle the correct letter.*)

   A. $\frac{9}{16} + \frac{2}{16} = \frac{7}{16}$　　　　**C.** $\frac{9}{16} + \frac{2}{16} = \frac{11}{32}$

   B. $\frac{9}{16} - \frac{2}{16} = \frac{7}{16}$　　　　**D.** $\frac{9}{16} + \frac{2}{16} = \frac{11}{16}$

2. The table below shows the fractions four friends wrote on the board. Which answer choice shows the fractions listed in order from least to greatest? (*Circle the correct letter.*)

Friend	Janet	Mary	Peggy	Margaret
Fraction	$\frac{5}{6}$	$\frac{3}{4}$	$\frac{1}{4}$	$\frac{2}{3}$

   A. $\frac{1}{4}$, $\frac{5}{6}$, $\frac{3}{4}$, $\frac{2}{3}$　　**B.** $\frac{1}{4}$, $\frac{5}{6}$, $\frac{2}{3}$, $\frac{3}{4}$　　**C.** $\frac{2}{3}$, $\frac{3}{4}$, $\frac{1}{4}$, $\frac{5}{6}$　　**D.** $\frac{1}{4}$, $\frac{2}{3}$, $\frac{3}{4}$, $\frac{5}{6}$

DAILY
Warm-Up 21

Name _Beling_

Date _____

1. Maci scored 400,000 plus 700 points on a board game. Ty scored one thousand, two hundred more points than Maci. Use arrows to show where Maci's and Ty's points fall on the number line below.

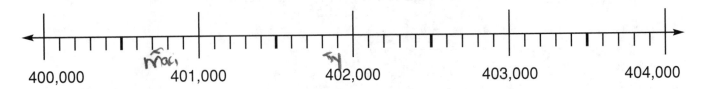

400,000   401,000   402,000   403,000   404,000

2. In Mrs. Jordon's class, 9 of the 30 students received A's on their projects. What fraction of the students received an A? (*Show your work and circle your final answer.*)

$$\frac{9}{30} = \frac{9 \div 3}{30 \div 3} = \boxed{\frac{3}{10}}$$ 9:30 2:4   0:12 $\frac{2}{4} \div 2 = \frac{1}{2}$

DAILY
Warm-Up 22

Name _Beling_

Date _____

1. Write each number below in standard form.

   A. 500,000,000 + 90,000,000 + 300,000 + 80,000
      + 5,000 + 900 + 2 = _590,385,902_   _590,385,902_

   B. Eight hundred sixty-three thousand,
      four hundred eighty-four =   _863,484_

   C. Three hundred sixty million, four hundred
      eighty-four thousand, nine hundred =   _360,484,900_

2. Use the greatest common factors of 30 and 45 to reduce the fraction below.

$$\frac{30 \div \boxed{15}}{45 \div \boxed{15}} = \frac{\boxed{2}}{\boxed{3}}$$

DAILY Warm-Up 23

Name _____ Date _____

1. When the students of Mr. Roddy's math class walked in the room this morning, the problem below was on the board as their warm-up. If the students did the problem correctly, what answer did they give?

> Write the prime factorization for the fraction, then reduce the fraction to the lowest terms.

$$\frac{54 =}{135 =} \underline{\hspace{3cm}} = \frac{\square}{\square}$$

2. One of Janet's math problems was to arrange the numbers below from greatest to least. If Janet did this correctly, what order did she write the numbers in?

| $\frac{3}{4}$ | 0.2 | $\frac{2}{5}$ | 0.25 | $\frac{1}{2}$ |

___ ___ ___ ___ ___

DAILY Warm-Up 24

Name _____ Date _____

1. Kurt swam $\frac{1}{4}$ of a mile on Monday, $1\frac{1}{4}$ miles on Tuesday, $2\frac{3}{4}$ miles on Wednesday, and $3\frac{1}{4}$ miles on Thursday. Which number line shows the correct number of miles Kurt swam during the 4-day period? (*Circle the correct letter.*)

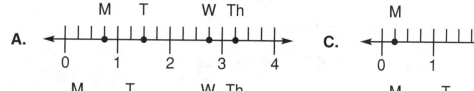

2. Look at the problem. Which symbol is needed to correctly compare the two fractions? (*Circle the correct letter.*)

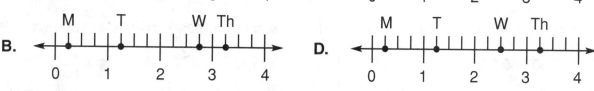

$$\frac{5}{9} \bigcirc \frac{1}{2}$$

A. >   **B.** <   **C.** =   **D.** Not Here

1. Fernando wrote the least common multiple of 6 and 8 on a piece of paper. He asked Charles if he could do the same. If Charles did the problem correctly, what answer did Charles give Fernando? (*Show your work and circle your final answer.*)

2. Jared is helping Mr. Mann feed his goats. Of the 90 goats on the farm, 36 of the goats are solid white. What percent of the goats on the farm are solid white? (*Show your work and circle your final answer.*)

1. Which is true about prime numbers? (*Circle the correct letter.*)

    A. A prime number has more than 1 and itself as a factor.

    B. A prime number has no factors.

    C. A prime number has only 1 and itself as factors.

    D. All prime numbers have 1, itself, and the number 4 as factors.

2. Which list shows the number in order from least to greatest? (*Circle the correct letter.*)

A. 850,230,298	750,839,792	550,120,673	450,742,903
B. 405,742,903	550,120,673	750,839,792	850,230,298
C. 450,742,903	850,230,298	750,839,792	550,120,673
D. 750,839,792	550,120,673	850,230,298	450,742,903

Name _____ **Date** _____

Warm-Up 27

1. At Roddy Auto World, if a person buys a car that costs $40,000 or more, they will receive a $5,000 rebate from the car company. If r stands for the money spent on a car, which answer choice matches the condition for earning the rebate? (*Circle the correct letter.*)

A. r ≤ 40,000

C. r ≥ 5,000

B. 5,000 ≥ r

D. r ≥ 40,000

2. Use your pencil to make 10 squares. With your pencil, shade in 7/10 of the squares. What percent of the squares are left? (*Show your work and circle your final answer.*)

Name _____ **Date** _____

Warm-Up 28

1. Look at each pair of figures below. Which figures are equivalent fractions? (*Circle the correct letter.*)

A.   **B.**   **C.**   **D.**

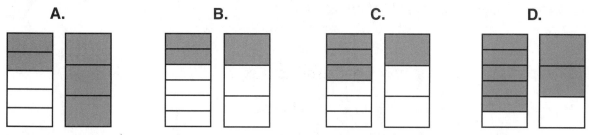

2. Lisa needs 96 quarts of frozen strawberries for the punch she is making. If she can only buy the frozen strawberries in 1-gallon containers, how many gallon containers should Lisa buy? (*Show your work and circle your final answer.*)

DAILY
Warm-Up 29

Name _____ Date _____

1. Travis found 14 pennies, 6 dimes, and 5 quarters on the floor of his bedroom. How is the fraction of quarters found written as a decimal? (*Show your work and circle your final answer.*)

2. Show the prime factorization of 240.

DAILY
Warm-Up 30

Name _____ Date _____

1. While walking on the beach, Timothy found 60 seashells in 3 hours. If the rate of Timothy finding seashells continues, how many seashells will Timothy find in 24 hours? (*Show your work and circle your final answer.*)

2. Look at the two decimal numbers below. Circle the decimal that is greater.

0.648   0.66

Name _____ **Date** _____

1. Look at the fractions below. Write them in order from **least to greatest.**

$$\frac{5}{8} \qquad \frac{3}{4} \qquad \frac{2}{3} \qquad \frac{1}{4}$$

_____ _____ _____ _____

2. Today, the weatherman called for a $\frac{3}{4}$ chance of rain. What percent names the chance of rain?

Name _____ **Date** _____

1. Look at the sets of numbers below. Find the **greatest common factor** for each set.

A. 12, 24, and 36 = ☐   **C.** 6, 12, and 14 = ☐

B. 18 and 27 = ☐   **D.** 15 and 35 ☐

2. Corrina and Pete are playing a numbers game. The models below represent the numbers each child has thus far. What number does Corrina need to draw to have a larger number than Pete and be able to win the game?

Corrina

| 2 | | 8 | , | 4 | 6 | 9 | , | 3 | 2 | 7 |

A. 5   **C.** 7

B. 6   **D.** 8

Pete

| 2 | 7 | 9 | , | 5 | 7 | 8 | , | 9 | 3 | 8 |

DAILY
Warm-Up 33

Name _____   Date _____

1. Hannah and Hank wrote the numbers below. If Hank switched the digit he wrote in the thousands place with the digit he wrote in the ten millions place, who would have the larger number, Hannah or Hank?

Hannah
9 5 3 , 6 4 2 , 8 7 0

Hank
9 1 2 , 3 4 6 , 2 8 7

Explain: _____

_____

_____

2. List all of the **factors** for the number 36.

- -

DAILY
Warm-Up 34

Name _____   Date _____

1. Arrange these numbers from **greatest to least**.

-2	$2\frac{1}{2}$	0	1	$1\frac{1}{4}$

_____ _____ _____ _____ _____

2. Mark told Sally to write two subtraction problems on a piece of paper and he would solve the problems. The problems below are what Sally wrote. If Mark answered correctly, what answers did he give?

A. 5 less than 2 = [   ]   **B.** 12 less than 7 = [   ]

Warm-Up 35

1. Find the product of 37 and 139. Then, round the product to the nearest thousand. (*Show your work and circle your final answer.*)

2. **A.** Joy ordered 4 boxes of stuffed animals for a dart-throwing game at the fair. Each box cost $89 and weighed more than 75 pounds. There were 50 stuffed animals in each box. Four-fifths of the stuffed animals were defective and had to be sent back. How many stuffed animals had to be sent back? (*Show your work and circle your final answer.*)

   B. Which two pieces of information are not needed in order to solve the question above?

   _____ and _____

- -

Warm-Up 36

1. Which statement is true about the numbers in the box? (*Circle the correct letter.*)

   A. The sum of the two numbers is 22.

   B. The sum of the two numbers is 0.

   C. The product of the two numbers is 0.

   D. not given

   $$+11 \text{ and } -11$$

2. Marshal wrote the number 48.7 in words on the chalk board of his classroom. Which number did Marshal write? (*Circle the correct letter.*)

   A. Four hundred eighty-seven

   B. Forty-eight and seven hundredths

   C. Forty-eight and seven tenths

   D. Forty-eight and seven thousandths

DAILY
Warm-Up 37

Name _____ **Date** _____

1. The table shows the times four runners finished the 40-yard dash. How many runners finished the race in more than 8.5 seconds? (*Circle the correct letter.*)

A. 1   **C.** 3

B. 2   **D.** 4

Runner	Time (sec.)
Brent	8.05
Scott	8.50
Katie	8.46
Tammy	8.63

2. Look at the model below. What percent of the squares are shaded? (*Circle your final answer.*)

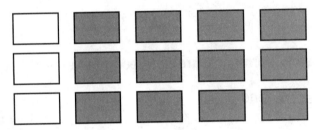

DAILY
Warm-Up 38

Name _____ **Date** _____

1. Chelsea wrote the digit 1 on the board. Which statement about the digit Chelsea wrote is true? (*Circle the correct letter.*)

   A. The digit is prime.

   B. The digit 1 is composite.

   C. The digit 1 is prime and composite.

   D. There are no factors for the digit 1.

2. Look at the expression below. What is the value of *n*? (*Circle your final answer.*)

$$7 + (-7) = n$$

Name _____ **Date** _____

1. The sixth-grade class is going fishing for their field trip. There are 360 bottles of water cooling in an ice cooler. There are 400 students in the sixth grade but only 90% showed up for the field trip. Are there enough bottles of water for the students going on the field trip? (*Show your work and circle your final answer.*)

2. Show the prime factorization of 360 using exponents.

Name _____ **Date** _____

1. Michael, Paige, and Sarah each wrote a number between 1 and 100. The table shows the number each person wrote. What is the greatest common factor for all three numbers? (*Show your work and circle your final answer.*)

Michael	72
Paige	36
Sarah	48

2. Louise and Ken walk each morning. They can walk 2 blocks in 4 minutes. If they continue to walk at the same pace, how many blocks could they walk in 32 minutes? (*Show your work and circle your final answer.*)

Warm-Up 41

1. Look at the pie chart. Which two regions represent **25%** of the circle? (*Circle the correct letter.*)

   A. W and Y   **C.** Y and X

   B. W and X   **D.** Z and X

   If you add regions W and Z, what percent of the circle would you get?

2. Look at the fractions below. List the fractions in order from **greatest to least**.

$$\frac{2}{3} \qquad \frac{3}{4} \qquad \frac{1}{2} \qquad \frac{1}{4} \qquad \frac{1}{8}$$

____ ____ ____ ____ ____

Warm-Up 42

1. Four students were asked to write only prime numbers on a sheet of paper. The table below shows the numbers each person wrote. Which student did this correctly?

Student	Prime Numbers
Sam	7, 23, 27, 42, 61
Ian	1, 5, 17, 31, 60
Hans	2, 13, 19, 43, 59
Kelly	2, 9, 17, 29, 53

2. What is the sum of the first seven positive, even numbers? (*Show your work and circle your final answer.*)

Name _____   **Date** _____

1. Sue has 120 pennies. 25% of the pennies are dated 1930, 25% of the pennies are dated 1920, and 50% are dated 1910. How many pennies of each date does Sue have? Write each answer in the table below.

Date	Number of Pennies
1930	
1920	
1910	

2. Four classmates had an assignment to make a 7-digit number that is divisible by 3. Which person did the assignment correctly? (*Circle the correct letter.*)

A. Kyle

B. Sandra

C. Michael

D. Jeffrey

Friend	Number
Jeffrey	687,096
Michael	1,587,039
Sandra	2,578,031
Kyle	1,687,093

Name _____   **Date** _____

1. Mary bought a package of buttons she plans to sew on a dress she is making. She wanted to place an equal number of buttons down each side of the dress. When she opened the package, she found that it was **not** possible. Which of the following could be the total number of buttons in the package Mary bought? (*Circle the correct letter.*)

A. 24   **B.** 28   **C.** 32   **D.** 35

2. Robin and Terry each bought a box of chocolate. There were 16 pieces of chocolate in each box. Robin now has $\frac{1}{4}$ of the pieces of chocolate left, and Terry has $\frac{1}{8}$ of the pieces of chocolate left. Which is true about the number of pieces of chocolate Robin and Terry have left? (*Circle the correct letter.*)

A. Robin has 14 pieces and Terry has 2 pieces left.

B. Robin has 4 pieces and Terry has none left.

C. Robin has 4 pieces and Terry has 2 pieces left.

D. Terry has more pieces of chocolate left than Robin.

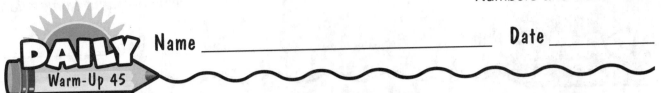

Name _____ **Date** _____

Warm-Up 45

1. Hank bought 20 sodas for his baseball team. Of the 20 sodas, 8 were strawberry flavored. What percent of the sodas was strawberry flavored? (*Show your work and circle your final answer.*)

2. Of the 100 members of the parent/teacher organization, 85 parents voted to purchase new playground equipment for the students at Dawson Elementary. What percent of the parents voted to purchase the equipment? (*Show your work and circle your final answer.*)

Name _____ **Date** _____

Warm-Up 46

1. Jennifer bought 2 packages of hair ribbons for $1.98 each, 2 boxes of Kleenex for $0.98 each, and 1 notebook for $1.97. What is the best estimate of the amount of money Jennifer spent on all items? (*Show your work and circle your final answer.*)

2. Joan drew the decimal numbers on the board. She asked Maria to find the sum of the decimal numbers represented by points A and B. If Maria found the correct answer, what answer did Maria get? (*Show your work and circle your final answer.*)

DAILY
Warm-Up 47

Name _____   Date _____

1. Doug drove 23.9 miles from his house to his farm, 18.3 miles from his farm to his field, 14.3 miles to pickup his daughter, and then 12.8 miles to get back home. What was the total number of miles Doug drove? Find your answer to the tenths place, and then bubble in the answer document. (*Show your work and circle your final answer.*)

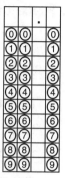

2. Marty is taking his math exam. There are 100 questions on the exam. Marty has $1\frac{1}{2}$ hours to complete the exam. When Marty's teacher graded his exam, he finds that Marty answered 60% of the questions correctly. How many questions did Marty answer correctly? Write this percentage as a reduced fraction. (*Show your work and circle your final answer.*)

- -

DAILY
Warm-Up 48

Name _____   Date _____

1. Round each number to the underlined digit.

   A. 0.3<u>0</u>4 _____   **F.** 5.<u>2</u>76 _____   **K.** 1.9<u>9</u>5 _____

   B. 2.13<u>5</u>6 _____   **G.** 15.9<u>6</u>4 _____   **L.** 0.85<u>4</u> _____

   C. 0.<u>2</u>78 _____   **H.** 1.4<u>9</u>7 _____   **M.** 4.<u>0</u>95 _____

   D. 0.<u>1</u>87 _____   **I.** 4.<u>5</u>24 _____   **N.** 5.6<u>4</u>8 _____

   E. 1.<u>9</u>74 _____   **J.** 3.0<u>5</u>8 _____   **O.** 6.<u>1</u>65 _____

2. Marco has 13 quarters, 16 nickels, 24 dimes, and 128 pennies in his piggy bank. He added that money to the $59.53 he had in his savings account. How much money does Marco now have in his savings account? (*Show your work and circle your final answer.*)

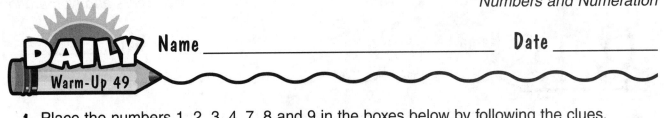

Name _____   **Date** _____

1. Place the numbers 1, 2, 3, 4, 7, 8 and 9 in the boxes below by following the clues.

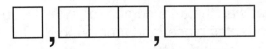

- The number is an odd number.
- The 1 has the greatest value.
- The 2 is in the hundreds place.
- The 4 is in the thousands place.
- The 9 has a greater place value than the 7.

- The lowest value has the second lowest odd number.
- The 8 belongs to the left of the 4.

2. Moses is trying to find the least common multiple of 6 and 8. When he couldn't find the answer, he asked Beth to help him. If Beth gave him the correct answer, what answer did Beth give? (*Circle the correct letter.*)

A. 12   **B.** 16   **C.** 24   **D.** 18

Name _____   **Date** _____

1. Place the numbers 1, 2, 5, 6, and 7 in the boxes below by following the clues.

- The number in the ten thousands place is 1.
- The number is an even number.
- The 2 is in the thousands place.
- The 7 has a larger value than the 5.

2. Tammy is ordering cups for her store. The ratio of small cups to large cups she has in the store is 12 to 10. If there are 40 large cups, how many small cups does Tammy have in stock? (*Show your work and circle your final answer.*)

Warm-Up 51

1. Which answer choice best represents the number 4,523,948? (*Circle the correct letter.*)

    A. 4 x 1,000,000 + 2 x 100,000 + 2 x 100,000 + 3 x 10,000 + 9 x 1,000 + 4 x 100 + 8 x 1

    B. 4 x 1,000,000 + 5 x 100,000 + 2 x 10.000 + 30 x 1,000 + 9 x 100 + 4 x 10 + 8 x 1

    C. 4 x 1,000,000 + 5 x 1,000,000 + 2 x 100,000 + 3 x 10,000 + 9 x 100 + 4 x 10 + 8 x 1

    D. 4 x 1,000,000 + 5 x 100,000 + 2 x 10,000 + 3 x 1,000 + 9 x 100 + 4 x 10 + 8 x 1

2. Beverly bought 3 pairs of jeans from Harold's Clothing. Each pair of jeans costs $59.98 (tax included). If Beverly writes a check, how much should she write the check for? Calculate the total price Beverly will pay and write it in the box. Then, write the amount of the check in words on the empty line.

Beverly Henderson 555 Station Avenue El Campo, TX 77437	CK #100
Pay to the order of _____ Harold's Clothing _____	$ [ ]
_____	
_____ Jeans _____	*Beverly Henderson*

Warm-Up 52

1. Show the prime factorization for the number 48 using exponents.

2. On Pete's first try, he scored 529,567,874 points playing a pinball machine. On his second try, Pete scored 528,567,874 points playing the same game. Which place value is important in determining on which try Pete scored the most points? (*Circle the correct letter.*)

    A. hundred thousands

    C. ten millions

    B. millions

    D. hundred millions

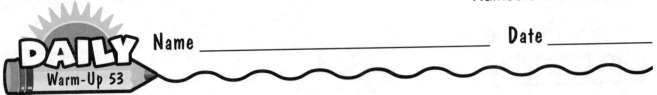

Name _____ **Date** _____

Warm-Up 53

1. Linda won 25 stuffed animals at the fair. She gave $\frac{3}{5}$ of the stuffed animals to her cousin. How many stuffed animals did Linda give her cousin? (*Show your work and circle your final answer.*)

2. At Burger World, one out of every 20 customers substituted their french fries for curly fries. What percent of the customers ordered curly fries? (*Show your work and circle your final answer.*)

- -

Name _____ **Date** _____

Warm-Up 54

1. At the high school basketball game, 24 out of every 100 spectators wore a baseball cap. What percent of the spectators wore baseball caps? (*Show your work and circle your final answer.*)

2. Twenty customers each had a coupon for a free car wash. Eight customers used their coupons before expiration date. What percent of the coupons were used? (*Show your work and circle your final answer.*)

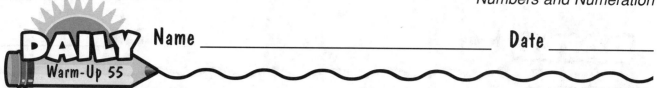

Name _____ Date _____

1. Cody bought a package of toy cars for his cousin. There were 4 toy cars in each package. The blue toy car was 1.9 cm long, the orange toy car was 2.136 cm long, the red toy car was 2.7 cm long, and the green toy car was 1.93 cm long. Which list below shows the color of these toy cars in order from the longest to the shortest in length? (*Circle the correct letter.*)

   A. blue, green, orange, red

   B. red, green, blue, orange

   C. orange, red, green, blue

   D. red, orange, green, blue

2. Maci threw 30 plastic rings to the bottom of her swimming pool. When she dove down, she retrieved 25 of the plastic rings. What is the ratio of plastic rings Maci retrieved to the number of plastic rings she threw to the bottom of the pool? (*Show your work and circle your final answer.*)

- -

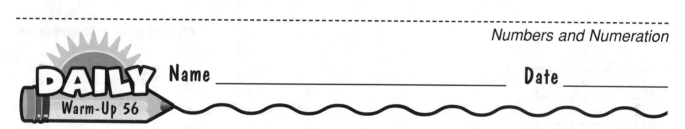

Name _____ Date _____

1. Show the prime factorization of 440 using exponents.

2. Yolanda bought a box of 60 colored tiles. She used $\frac{1}{3}$ of the tiles making a mosaic table. She gave $\frac{1}{5}$ of the tiles to her friend Jane. How many colored tiles does Yolanda have left in the box? (*Show your work and circle your final answer.*)

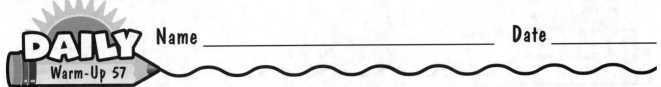

DAILY
Warm-Up 57

Name _____   Date _____

1. Jared has $147.86 in his piggy bank. He received $60 for his birthday and earned $25 for mowing his neighbor's lawn. He deposited all the money he had at home into his savings account, where he already had a balance of $587.93. Jared is saving to buy a new computer that cost $1,980.99 including tax. How much more money does Jared need to save so he can buy the computer he wants? (*Show your work and circle your final answer.*)

2. Mike hauls oranges from Florida to other states 7 days a week. Mike drives 9 hours each day. Mike's average speed is 70 miles per hour. At this rate, how many miles will Mike drive in 7 days? (*Show your work and circle your final answer.*)

DAILY
Warm-Up 58

Name _____   Date _____

1. Which are prime factors for the number 180 using exponents? (*Circle the correct letter.*)

   A. 2, 5^4, and 7

   B. 2 x 3 x 5

   C. 2, 5, and 7

   D. 2^2 x 3^2 x 5

2. The table shows the amount of tickets sold by four friends. Which friend sold the most tickets? (*Circle the correct letter.*)

   A. Carlos   **C.** Anthony

   B. Mandy   **D.** Laura

Name	Tickets Sold
Carlos	$\frac{3}{6}$
Anthony	$\frac{1}{10}$
Mandy	$\frac{2}{10}$
Laura	$\frac{1}{5}$

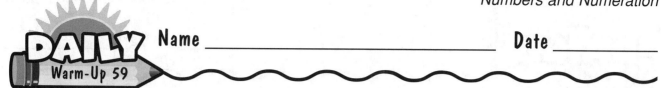

Name _____ **Date** _____

1. Which number sentence is true? (*Circle the correct letter.*)

A. $1.4 < 1\frac{40}{100}$ **B.** $2.74 > 2\frac{77}{100}$ **C.** $.4 > \frac{42}{100}$ **D.** $2.5 < 2\frac{59}{100}$

2. Martin bought 3.15 pounds of hamburger meat for a barbeque. He already had 4.5 pounds in his freezer at home. How many total pounds of hamburger meat does Martin now have for the barbeque? (*Show your work and circle your final answer.*)

Name _____ **Date** _____

1. Use your pencil to shade in three and four hundredths.

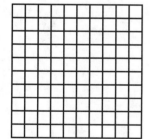 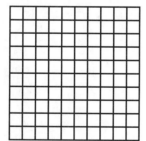 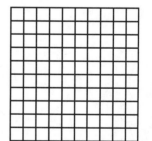 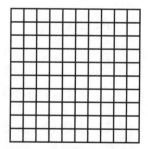

2. The table shows the number of inches of rain that fell during a 7-day period in El Campo, Texas. On which day was the greatest amount of rain reported? (*Circle the correct letter.*)

A. Thursday   **C.** Saturday

B. Friday   **D.** Sunday

Day	Rain
Sunday	3.29
Monday	7.16
Tuesday	3.27
Wednesday	8.37
Thursday	8.47
Friday	7.6
Saturday	4.9

Name _____   **Date** _____

Warm-Up 61

1. The prime factorization of a number is 2×3^4. Which of the choices below is the number? (*Circle the correct letter.*)

   A. 168

   B. 162

   C. 184

   D. 199

2. Solve the problems below. Write each answer in lowest terms.

   A. $\frac{7}{12} + \frac{3}{12} = \dfrac{\square}{\square}$

   B. $\frac{14}{25} - \frac{5}{25} = \dfrac{\square}{\square}$

   C. $\frac{2}{8} + \frac{3}{8} = \dfrac{\square}{\square}$

   D. $\frac{5}{9} - \frac{4}{9} = \dfrac{\square}{\square}$

   E. $\frac{5}{10} + \frac{3}{10} = \dfrac{\square}{\square}$

   F. $\frac{9}{15} - \frac{4}{15} = \dfrac{\square}{\square}$

   G. $\frac{1}{8} + \frac{3}{8} = \dfrac{\square}{\square}$

   H. $\frac{3}{5} - \frac{2}{5} = \dfrac{\square}{\square}$

   I. $\frac{2}{7} + \frac{3}{7} = \dfrac{\square}{\square}$

Name _____   **Date** _____

Warm-Up 62

1. Which of the following shows the prime factorization of 680? (*Circle the correct letter.*)

   A. $2 \times 5 \times 17$

   B. $2 \times 3 \times 5 \times 17$

   C. $2 \times 3 \times 5 \times 5 \times 17$

   D. $2 \times 2 \times 2 \times 5 \times 17$

2. The table below shows the fraction of the total amount of boxes of candy bars sold by four friends. Which of the following friends sold the most candy bars? (*Circle the correct letter.*)

   A. George

   B. Tim

   C. Mark

   D. Tammy

Name	Boxes Sold
George	$\frac{1}{4}$
Tim	$\frac{2}{5}$
Mark	$\frac{1}{5}$
Tammy	$\frac{3}{20}$

Answer Key

Warm-Up 1
1. 80% A; 20% B
2. 27 fish

Warm-Up 2
1. A. >
   B. =
   C. <
2. You should multiply 120 by 0.90.

Warm-Up 3
1. 28
2. B

Warm-Up 4
1. $3\frac{1}{4}$ inches
2. $\frac{5}{6}$ of the tickets

Warm-Up 5
1. C
2. $2^3 \times 3^2$; Possible factor tree:

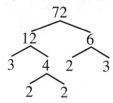

Warm-Up 6
1. $\frac{4}{8}$ is greater; after reducing, $\frac{4}{16}$ becomes $\frac{1}{4}$ and $\frac{4}{8}$ becomes $\frac{1}{2}$. $\frac{1}{2}$ is greater than $\frac{1}{4}$.
2.

Warm-Up 7
1. D
2. D

Warm-Up 8
1. C
2. C

Warm-Up 9
1. 0.6
2. $4\frac{1}{4}$ feet

Warm-Up 10
1. A   2. C

Warm-Up 11
1. C   2. B

Warm-Up 12
1. 668 decorations
2. 45 flowers

Warm-Up 13
1. B
2. $\frac{6}{8}$

Warm-Up 14
1. $\frac{1}{4}, \frac{2}{6}, \frac{1}{2}, \frac{2}{3}, \frac{3}{4}$
2. 24.5

Warm-Up 15
1. C
2. 6 : 11

Warm-Up 16
1. A
2. 6 square inches

Warm-Up 17
1. The integer +2 is greater.

2. Henry has 12 cards left. Deron has 3 cards left.

Warm-Up 18
1. C
2. 60 baseball cards

Warm-Up 19
1. 80 cars
2. B

Warm-Up 20
1. B
2. D

Warm-Up 21
1. Maci: 400,700
   Ty: 401,900

2. $\frac{3}{10}$

Warm-Up 22
1. A. 590,385,902
   B. 863,484
   C. 360,484,900
2. $\frac{2}{3}$

Warm-Up 23
1. $\frac{54}{135} = \frac{2 \times 3 \times 3 \times 3}{3 \times 3 \times 3 \times 5} = \frac{2}{5}$
2. $\frac{3}{4}, \frac{1}{2}, \frac{2}{5}$, 0.25, 0.2

Warm-Up 24
1. B
2. A

Warm-Up 25
1. 24
2. 40%

Warm-Up 26
1. C
2. B

Warm-Up 27
1. D
2. 30%

Warm-Up 28
1. B
2. 24 gallons

Warm-Up 29
1. 0.2
2. $2^4 \times 3 \times 5$

Warm-Up 30
1. 480 seashells
2. 0.66

Warm-Up 31
1. $\frac{1}{4}, \frac{5}{8}, \frac{2}{3}, \frac{3}{4}$
2. 75%

Warm-Up 32
1. A. 12
   B. 9
   C. 2
   D. 5
2. D

Answer Key

Warm-Up 33
1. Hank would have the larger number. The 6 he now has in the ten millions place is larger than the 5 Hannah has in the ten millions place.
2. 1, 2, 3, 4, 6, 9, 12, 18, 36

Warm-Up 34
1. $2\frac{1}{2}$, $1\frac{1}{4}$, 1, 0, -2
2. A. –3   B. –5

Warm-Up 35
1. 5,000
2. A. 160 stuffed animals
   B. cost and weight

Warm-Up 36
1. B
2. C

Warm-Up 37
1. A
2. 80%

Warm-Up 38
1. D
2. 0

Warm-Up 39
1. Yes. There is just enough for every student to have exactly 1 bottle of water.
2. 2^3 x 3^2 x 5

Warm-Up 40
1. 12
2. 16 blocks

Warm-Up 41
1. C; 75%
2. $\frac{3}{4}, \frac{2}{3}, \frac{1}{2}, \frac{1}{4}, \frac{1}{8}$

Warm-Up 42
1. Hans
2. 56

Warm-Up 43
1.
Date	Number of Pennies
1930	30
1920	30
1910	60

2. C

Warm-Up 44
1. D   2. C

Warm-Up 45
1. 40%
2. 85%

Warm-Up 46
1. $8.00
2. 6.6

Warm-Up 47
1.
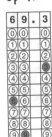

2. 60 questions; $\frac{3}{5}$

Warm-Up 48
1. A. 0.30   I. 4.5
   B. 2.136   J. 3.06
   C. 0.3   K. 2.00
   D. 0.2   L. 0.85
   E. 2.0   M. 4.1
   F. 5.3   N. 5.65
   G. 15.96   O. 6.2
   H. 1.50
2. $67.26

Warm-Up 49
1. 1,984,273
2. C

Warm-Up 50
1. 12,756
2. 48 small cups

Warm-Up 51
1. D
2. $179.94; One hundred seventy-nine dollars and 94 cents

Warm-Up 52
1. 2^4 x 3   2. B

Warm-Up 53
1. 15 stuffed animals
2. 5%

Warm-Up 54
1. 24%
2. 40%

Warm-Up 55
1. D   2. 5:6

Warm-Up 56
1. 2^3 x 5 x 11
2. 28 left

Warm-Up 57
1. $1,160.20
2. 4,410 miles

Warm-Up 58
1. D   2. A

Warm-Up 59
1. D
2. 7.65 lbs.

Warm-Up 60
1.

2. A

Warm-Up 61
1. B
2. A. $\frac{5}{6}$
   B. $\frac{9}{25}$
   C. $\frac{5}{8}$
   D. $\frac{1}{9}$
   E. $\frac{4}{5}$
   F. $\frac{1}{3}$
   G. $\frac{1}{2}$
   H. $\frac{1}{5}$
   I. $\frac{5}{7}$

Warm-Up 62
1. D   2. B

OPERATIONS

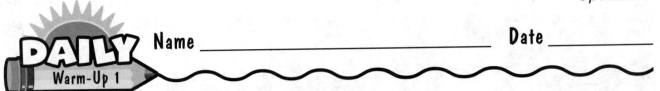

Name _____   Date _____

1. Mrs. Harrison ordered 3 packages of gold stars for a reading project she is doing with her students. If 3 packages of gold stars are enough for 15 students, how many packages does Mrs. Harrison need if she has 60 students doing the same project? (*Show your work and circle your final answer.*)

2. Jerry owns a furniture shop. During the month of March, the ratio of washing machines sold to refrigerators sold was 3:1. If there were 492 refrigerators sold, how many washing machines did Jerry sell? (*Show your work and circle your final answer.*)

- -

Name _____   Date _____

1. What are the common factors of 24 and 32? What is the greatest common factor of these two numbers? (*Show your work and circle your final answer.*)

2. Which statement below is **true** about exponents? (*Circle the correct letter.*)

   A. An exponent is the square root of the base number.

   B. An exponent is the number of times the base number is used as a factor.

   C. An exponent always has an equal value to the base number.

   D. An exponent does not show the number of times the base number is used as a factor.

1. Show the prime factorization of 72 using exponents. (*Show your work and circle your final answer.*)

2. Find the prime factorization for the number 48 by completing the factor tree.

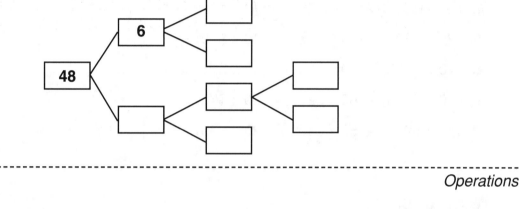

1. Look at the fractions below. Which fraction is the greatest? Which fraction is the least? (*Circle and label your answers.*)

$$\frac{5}{6} \qquad \frac{5}{9} \qquad \frac{2}{3} \qquad \frac{5}{12}$$

2. The mixed numbers below are what Chandler and Joseph wrote on the board. Who wrote the greater mixed number? (*Circle your final answer.*)

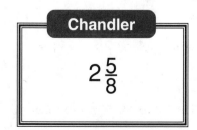

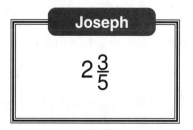

Name _____ **Date** _____

Warm-Up 5

1. Jenny's Flower Mart ordered 12 cases of carnations. Each case had 980 carnations. How many total carnations did Jenny order altogether? (*Circle the correct letter.*)

   A. 11,781   **B.** 11,968   **C.** 12,992   **D.** 11,760

2. Mary owns 120 rare stamps. Forty of the stamps are worth $200 each, 60 stamps are worth $150 each, and the rest of the stamps are worth $75 each. Which number sentence below can be used to find the amount of money Mary will make if she sells all 120 stamps? (*Circle the correct letter.*)

   A. (20 x $200) + (60 x $150) + (40 x $75) =

   B. (40 x $150) + (60 x $200) + (20 x $75) =

   C. (40 x $200) + (60 x $200) + (20 x $75) =

   D. (40 x $200) + (60 x $150) + (20 x $75) =

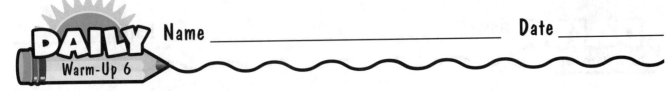

Name _____ **Date** _____

Warm-Up 6

1. If you are trying to find the quotient in a problem, you are using _____ . (*Circle the correct letter.*)

   A. addition   **B.** subtraction   **C.** multiplication   **D.** division

2. Henry and Sam entered a recycling contest. Henry recycled 459 cans. Sam recycled 324 more cans than Henry. How many more cans must Sam recycle to reach his goal of 1,700 cans? (*Show your work and circle your final answer.*)

Name _____   **Date** _____

1. Lee planted 78 rows of red onions. Each row has 109 onion plants. He also planted 98 rows of white onions with 146 onion plants in each row. Which expression can be used to find how many onion plants the farmer planted altogether? (*Circle the correct letter.*)

   A. $(78 \div 109) + (98 + 146)$ **C.** $(109 - 78) - (146 \times 98)$

   B. $(78 \times 109) + (146 - 98)$ **D.** $(109 \times 78) + (146 \times 98)$

2. The table shows the number of hours Heath will work at his new job this week. If Heath earns $7.50 for each hour worked, how much total money will Heath earn before taxes are taken out? (*Show your work and circle your final answer.*)

Day	Mon.	Tue.	Wed.	Thur.	Fri.	Sat.	Sun.
Hours Worked	7	6	Day Off	8	Day Off	12	10

- -

Name _____   **Date** _____

1. Solve the multiplication problems.

   A.   8 4 6   **B.**   6 5 6   **C.**   7 9 9
          x 8 4 6   x 7 7 5   x 3 0 6

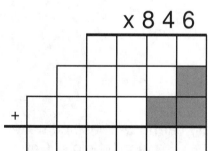

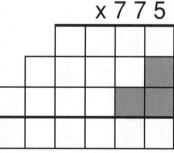

2. Carl wrote one of the problems below on the board for Greg to solve. If Greg found a correct quotient of 568, which problem did Carl write? (*Circle the correct letter.*)

   A. $9656 \div 15 =$ **B.** $9656 \div 16 =$ **C.** $9656 \div 17 =$ **D.** $9656 \div 18 =$

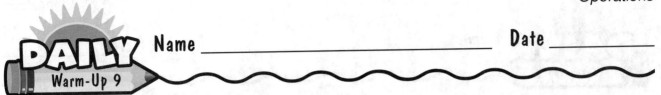

DAILY Warm-Up 9

1. Scott ordered 34 cases of cups for his store. Each case cost $75. When the order arrived, only 10 cases of medium cups and 15 cases of large cups came in. If Scott had to pay for the order that came in, how much did Scott pay for the cups? (*Show your work and circle your final answer.*)

2. For the school event, 112 tables were set up for students. Seventy-five of these tables could seat 8 students each, 25 of these tables could seat 6 students each, and the rest of the tables could seat 4 students each. If students are occupying all but 28 of the chairs, how many students are sitting down at the tables? (*Show your work and circle your final answer.*)

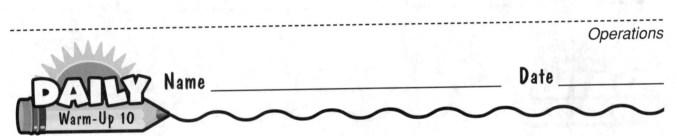

DAILY Warm-Up 10

1. Show the prime factorization for the number 400 without using exponents. (*Show your work and circle your final answer.*)

2. Chris cleans cars for extra money. He charges $32 for every car he washes and waxes. During the month of April, Chris washed and waxed 56 cars. The month before, Chris washed and waxed 25 fewer cars than he did in April. How much more money did Chris earn in April than in March? (*Show your work and circle your final answer.*)

1. At Hansen Elementary, there are 12 6th-grade classes. Each class has 35 students. For the camp fundraiser, if every 6th-grade student sells 18 boxes of candy bars, how many total boxes will the 6th-grade students sell? (*Show your work and circle your final answer.*)

2. At a book store, Lee and his two sisters bought 3 books for $4 each, 3 book markers for $.89 each, and 3 magazines for $2 each. If they decide to split the cost evenly, which equation below can be used to find *m*, the amount of money each person will need to pay, excluding tax, for their part of the expense? (*Circle the correct letter.*)

A. [(3 + 4) + (.89 x 3) + (3 x 2)] ÷ 3 = *m*   **C.** [(3 x 4) + (.89 x 3) + (3 x 4)] ÷ 3 = *m*

B. [(4 − 3) + (.89 + 3) + (3 x 2)] ÷ 3 = *m*   **D.** [(3 x 4) + (.89 x 3) + (3 x 2)] ÷ 3 = *m*

1. Look at the proportions below. Which proportion is **not** true?

A. $\frac{5}{6} = \frac{20}{24}$ **C.** $\frac{4}{8} = \frac{8}{16}$

B. $\frac{8}{12} = \frac{24}{36}$ **D.** $\frac{5}{15} = \frac{15}{30}$

2. In Mrs. Hubenak's math class, the class is taking a survey of how many students like having pizza in the cafeteria. If there are 32 students in the class and each student asks 25 people, how many total people will be surveyed? (*Show your work and circle your final answer.*)

Name _____ **Date** _____

Warm-Up 13

1. What is the correct definition of a common factor? (*Circle the correct letter.*)

    A. a factor shared by one number

    B. the bottom number in a fraction

    C. a factor shared by two or more numbers

    D. the top number in a fraction

2. Circle the expressions below where exponents are used correctly to make the number sentences true.

$$3^3 = 2 \times 3 \qquad 4^2 = 4 \times 4 \qquad 6^2 = 9 \times 4$$

$$3^2 = 3 \times 3 \qquad 5^2 = 2 \times 5 \qquad 7^2 = 2 \times 7$$

Name _____ **Date** _____

Warm-Up 14

1. Jim bought a new drill that was on sale for 30% off of the retail cost of the drill. The retail cost of the drill Jim bought including tax was $75. If Jim paid with a $100 bill, how much money did he receive back? (*Show your work and circle your final answer.*)

2. The science test Charles took this week had 60 questions. Charles answered 85% of the questions correctly. Last week, Charles took a test in the same class with the same number of questions on the test. During the test, he answered only 70% of the questions correctly. How many more questions did Charles answer correct on this week's test than on last week's test? (*Show your work and circle your final answer.*)

Name _____ **Date** _____

Warm-Up 15

1. Solve the problems below.

A. $\dfrac{1}{8}$ + $\dfrac{1}{16}$ **B.** $\dfrac{6}{9}$ − $\dfrac{2}{9}$ **C.** $\dfrac{3}{9}$ + $\dfrac{5}{18}$ **D.** $\dfrac{1}{2}$ − $\dfrac{3}{7}$ **E.** $\dfrac{2}{5}$ + $\dfrac{3}{10}$ **F.** $\dfrac{4}{6}$ − $\dfrac{2}{12}$

2. Show the prime factorization for the number 63 using exponents. (Show your work and circle your final answer.)

Name _____ **Date** _____

Warm-Up 16

1. David worked the problem below but can't find his mistake. Where did David go wrong? Circle David's mistake and correct it.

Step 1	Step 2	Step 3
$ 63 + $ 21 —— $ 84	$ 100 + $ 84 —— $ 184	184 ÷ 8 = 24

2. Jason multiplied two of the numbers below and got a product of 4,375. Which two numbers did he multiply? (*Circle your final answer.*)

A. 128 and 38   **B.** 127 and 37   **C.** 126 and 36   **D.** 125 and 35

Name _____ **Date** _____

Warm-Up 17

1. Melanie gave Gordon the clues in the box below so that he can guess the dividend to the division problem. Did Melanie give Gordon enough clues to find the answer? If so, what is the dividend? (*Show your work and circle your final answer.*)

> *If the divisor is 35 and the quotient is 56, what is the dividend?*

2. Mrs. Simpson asked her students to find the quotient when the sum of 24 and 12 is divided by the difference of 18 and 14. If his students answered correctly, what answer did they give? (*Show your work and circle your final answer.*)

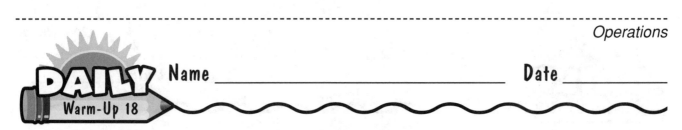

Name _____ **Date** _____

Warm-Up 18

1. Jennifer ordered 4 boxes of cookies. There were 48 cookies in the first box, 36 cookies in the second box, 24 cookies in the third box, and 12 cookies in the fourth box. If all the cookies were placed in four different boxes so that there were an equal number of cookies in each box, how many cookies would be in each box? (*Show your work and circle your final answer.*)

2. What is **true** about the number 675? (*Circle the correct letter.*)

A. It is divisible by 6 and 2.

C. It is divisible by 8 and 4.

B. It is divisible by 7 and 3.

D. It is divisible by 9 and 5.

Name _____ **Date** _____

Warm-Up 19

1. What is the product of the sum of 9 and 4 and the difference of 9 and 4? (*Show your work and circle your final answer.*)

2. At a gift shop, 270 baskets were being sent to soldiers overseas. Each basket held 15 packages of different types of candy. How many packages of candy will be needed for all 270 baskets? (*Show your work and circle your final answer.*)

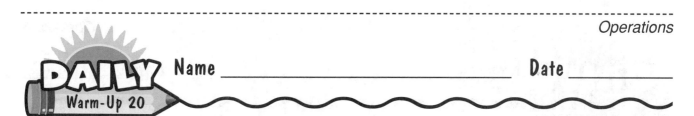

Name _____ **Date** _____

Warm-Up 20

1. Hannah, Sarah, and Olivia are measuring the weight of their dogs. Hannah's dog is twice as heavy as Sarah's dog but 5 pounds heavier than Olivia's dog. Olivia's dog weighs 35 pounds. How much do Hannah's and Sarah's dogs weigh? (*Show your work and circle your final answer.*)

2. Lucy baked some cookies for a bake sale. She baked 12 dozen cookies with each cookie weighing exactly 3 ounces. She carried the cookies in 3 large containers that weighing 4 pounds each. How much did all 3 containers of cookies weigh (in ounces and in pounds) after Lucy put the cookies inside? (*Show your work and circle your final answers.*)

1. Jerry has 452 watermelons he plans to sell at his watermelon stand. One hundred seventy-eight large watermelons sold for $12 each. One hundred eighty-three medium watermelons sold for $10 each. The remaining watermelons were small and sold for $8 each. How much total money did Jerry make selling his watermelons? (*Show your work and circle your final answer.*)

2. **A.** At Scott's store, he has 15 cases of different types of jelly. Each case has 14 rows with 12 jars of jelly in each row. Each jar of jelly sells for $4.49 each. How many total jars of jelly does Scott have in all 15 cases? (*Show your work and circle your final answer.*)

   B. What information given above is not needed to solve the question?

---

1. Mrs. Mann is collecting donations for a school that flooded. Altogether, 2,970 packages of markers were donated by the community. If she can pack 35 packages of markers in each box, how many total boxes will Mrs. Mann need to mail all 2,970 packages of markers? (*Show your work and circle your final answer.*)

2. At the local elementary school, the 4th-, 5th-, and 6th-grade classes are having a bake sale. Each grade level has 250 bags of cookies with a dozen cookies in each bag for sale. When the bake sale was over, 4,560 cookies were left over. How many total cookies were sold at the bake sale? How many total bags of cookies were left over? (*Show your work and circle your final answers.*)

Name _____ **Date** _____

1. Linda works at a dress shop. In Saturday's shipment, 396 dresses came in that needed to be hung on 12 different racks. If Linda hung an equal number of dresses on each rack, how many dresses did she hang on each rack? (*Show your work and circle your final answer.*)

2. At Terry's birthday, she had 52 party favors for her guests. She handed an equal number of party favors to each of her 4 guests. Terry then had 24 party favors left over. How many party favors did each guest receive? (*Show your work and circle your final answer.*)

Name _____ **Date** _____

1. Jason is planning his family's reunion at a water park. A total of 30 family members are coming. There are 18 adults attending, and the rest are children. How much money is needed for all 30 family members to attend the water park (not including tax)? (*Show your work and circle your final answer.*)

| Admit One Adult $25.95 | Admit One Child $18.95 |

2. There are 5 players playing a board game. If a player lands on the "Game Over" square, he or she is out of the game and must divide his or her winnings evenly among the other players. When Andrew landed on that square, he had accumulated $3,248. How much money will each player receive from him? (*Show your work and circle your final answer.*)

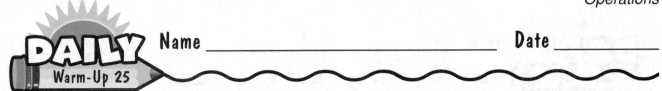

Warm-Up 25

1. There are 30 students in the choir at Gold Elementary. One-third of the students are 6th-graders and the rest are 5th-graders. Of the 6th-graders in choir, one-fifth won first place in the choir concert this summer. How many 6th-grade students won first place in the choir concert? (*Show your work and circle your final answer.*)

2. Marsha emptied her piggy bank. She had 12 one-dollar bills, 8 ten-dollar bills, and 2 twenty-dollar bills. She also had 76 quarters, 120 dimes, 94 nickels, and 429 pennies. How much money has Marsha saved in her piggy bank? (*Show your work and circle your final answer.*)

Warm-Up 26

1. Robin needs help making decorations. She agreed to pay her sister $5, plus an additional $0.25 for every decoration she makes. Robin paid her sister $15.25 for her help. How many decorations did Robin's sister make? (*Circle the correct letter.*)

A. 61   **B.** 51   **C.** 41   **D.** 31

2. Mandy wrote the number 4658.2 on the board. Mark wrote a number that was 568.09 greater than Mandy's number. What number did Mark write? (*Show your work and circle your final answer.*)

Warm-Up 27

1. What is the least common multiple of 7, 6, and 2? (*Show your work and circle your final answer.*)

2. Jessica went to the mall and bought 3 shirts for $12 each and 3 hats for $8 each. Which expression represents the total cost of Jessica's purchases? (*Circle the correct letter.*)

A. (3 x $3) + (12 x $8)

C. (3 x $12) + (3 x $8)

B. (3 x $12) + (8 – $3)

D. (3 + $12) + (3 + $8)

- -

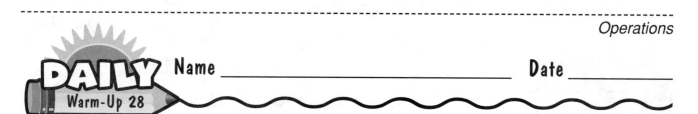

Warm-Up 28

1. Three friends plan to purchase 12 horses for $1,096 each. If the three friends plan to share the cost equally, how much money will each friend owe? (*Show your work and circle your final answer.*)

2. Mrs. Watkins ordered four boxes of pencils for the new school year. There were 12 pencils in the first box, 24 pencils in the second box, 36 pencils in the third box, and 48 pencils in the fourth box. When the pencils arrived, if Mrs. Watkins took all the pencils out and placed an equal number of pencils back in each box, how many pencils would be in each box? (*Show your work and circle your final answer.*)

Name _____   **Date** _____

Warm-Up 29

1. At a track meet, Marco threw the shot put 35 yards, 30 yards, and 37 yards. Find Marco's average distances of throws. (*Show your work and circle your final answer.*)

2. Solve the multiplication problems below.

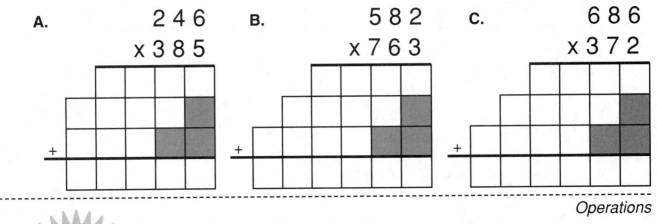

A. 2 4 6
    x 3 8 5

B. 5 8 2
    x 7 6 3

C. 6 8 6
    x 3 7 2

Name _____   **Date** _____

Warm-Up 30

1. At the cheerleading awards, 40% of the cheerleaders were awarded trophies for their participation throughout the year. If 18 cheerleaders were given trophies, how many total cheerleaders are on the team? (*Show your work and circle your final answer.*)

2. Corrina went shopping at Roddy's World. She bought 3 new music CDs for $18.89 each, 3 new books for $12.56 each, and 3 new shirts for $18.98 each. The tax came to $27.56. Find the total cost Corrina had to pay, and complete the check for her.

Corrina Jenson   Check #523
3333 East Lane
Victoria, MI 77482
Pay to the Order of _____ $ [   ]

_____

(Z) Zebra Banking
    10209, South TX
                                              _____
                                                Signature

Name _____ **Date** _____

1. Forty percent of the players on the high-school baseball team are seniors. If 20 players on the team are seniors, how many total students make up the baseball team? (*Show your work and circle your final answer.*)

2. Solve the division problems below.

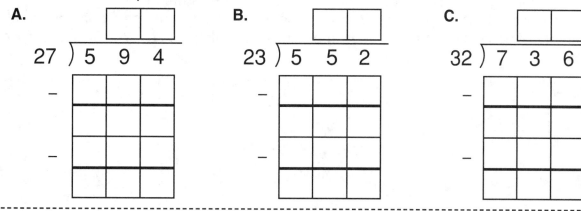

A. 27) 5 9 4

B. 23) 5 5 2

C. 32) 7 3 6

Name _____ **Date** _____

1. When students in Mrs. Hubbard's class walked into the room Monday morning, the problem below was written on the board. Show how the students worked the problem correctly. (*Show your work and circle your final answer.*)

> *Show the prime factorization for the number 400.*

2. Fernando owns a tire station. He charges $18 for every tire he fixes. During the month of January, Fernando fixed 106 tires. The month before, Fernando fixed 38 fewer tires than he did in January. How much total money did Fernando earn in the two months altogether? (*Show your work and circle your final answer.*)

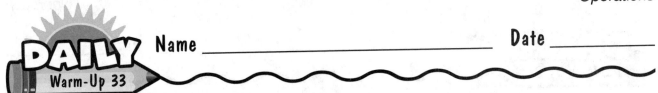

Name _____ **Date** _____

1. For every 8 laps Janet swam during swimming practice, Margo only swam 7. If Janet swam 48 laps during practice, how many laps did Margo swim? (*Circle the correct letter.*)

A. 48   **B.** 46   **C.** 44   **D.** 42

2. Coach Jon is putting basketball jerseys into plastic containers for storage. Each container can hold 24 jerseys. Which number sentence can be used to find the total number of containers that he needs in order to store all 96 jerseys? (*Circle the correct letter.*)

A. 96 x 12 = ☐

C. 96 ÷ 24 = ☐

B. 96 + ☐ = 24

D. ☐ − 12 = 96

Name _____ **Date** _____

Warm-Up 34

1. Solve the problems below.

A.

434,569
− 15,692

B.

96 ⟌ 3456

C.

957
x 887

D.

176,950
+ 195,398

2. Two-fifths of the 6th-grade students voted for class president. If there were 150 students that voted, how many students are in 6th grade? (*Show your work and circle your final answer.*)

Name _____   **Date** _____

Warm-Up 35

1. Daniel ordered 54 cases of oil for his store. Each case had 254 bottles of oil. Thirty-eight cases were a high grade of oil and the rest were a lower grade of oil. Each case of high-grade oil costs $225, and each case of lower-grade oil costs $150. When the order came in, only 19 cases of high-grade oil and 9 cases of lower-grade oil came in. If Daniel only had to pay for the cases that came in, how much did Daniel pay for the order that arrived at his store? (*Show your work and circle your final answer.*)

2. Colton had $\frac{8}{10}$ of a chocolate cake in his refrigerator when he left for work. When he arrived home, there was only $\frac{3}{10}$ of the cake left. What fraction describes the amount of cake that was eaten while Colton was at work? (*Show your work and circle your final answer.*)

Name _____   **Date** _____

Warm-Up 36

1. Robert collects valuable football cards. He has 204 football cards in his collection that were given to him by his dad. One-sixth of the football cards are worth $200 each. Half of the remaining football cards are worth $150 each, and the other half are worth $100 each. How much could Robert make by selling the cards that are worth $150 each? (*Show your work and circle your final answer.*)

2. Taylor is playing a card game with his friend. At the end of the first round, Taylor's friend had a score of 45 points and Taylor had a score of 27 points. At the end of the second round, Taylor's friend had 56 points, and Taylor had a score of –12. How many total points did Taylor lose at the end of the second round? (*Show your work and circle your final answer.*)

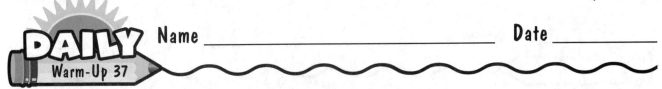

Name _____ Date _____

1. Jim bought 3 books for $18.64 each, 2 magazines for $3.99 each, and 4 music CDs for $15.79 each. Which expression shows how to find the total cost Jim spent altogether? (*Circle the correct letter.*)

   A. (3 x $18.64) + (2 x $3.99) + $15.79 = ☐

   B. (3 x $18.64) + (2 x $3.99) + (3 x $15.79) = ☐

   C. (3 x $18.64) + (2 x $3.99) + (4 x $15.79) = ☐

   D. (2 x $18.64) + (4 x $3.99) + (3 x $15.79) = ☐

2. Luke wants to buy an entertainment center. The entertainment center Luke wants costs $1,958.90. He has $250 in his savings account and deposits $100 into his account each month. How many months will it take Luke to save the money needed to purchase the entertainment center he wants? (*Show your work and circle your final answer.*)

Name _____ Date _____

1. What is the sum of the first 10 positive odd numbers? (*Show your work and circle your final answer.*)

2. At Orange Middle School, the 6th-grade student council is selling lollipops as a fundraiser. When their order of lollipops arrived, there were only 360 lollipops. There are 500 students at Orange Middle School. If 80% of them want to buy a lollipop, will the student council have enough for these students? (*Show your work and circle your final answer.*)

Circle: Yes or No

   Why or why not?_____

Name _____ **Date** _____

Warm-Up 39

1. At the movie theater, there are four different movies playing at the same time. There are 680 seats in each theater. 35% of the seats were filled in the 1st theater, 60% of the seats were filled in the 2nd theater, 45% of the seats were filled in the 3rd theater, and 80% of the seats were filled in the 4th theater. How many total people watched a movie at the same time? (*Show your work and circle your final answer.*)

2. Doreen is buying hay for her cattle. She bought 16,887 bails of hay that she wants to store in 3 separate barns. If Doreen divides the hay equally among each barn, how many bails will be stored in each barn? (*Circle the correct letter.*)

A. 6,529   **B.** 5,629   **C.** 4,629   **D.** 3,629

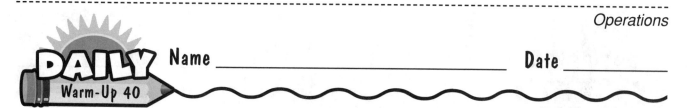

Name _____ **Date** _____

Warm-Up 40

1. Janice wants to buy 3 hamburgers for her 2 friends and herself. Each hamburger costs $2.90. She also wants to buy 3 drinks that cost $1.80 each. If tax is 8.5%, how much is Janice going to pay for the hamburgers and drinks? (*Show your work and circle your final answer.*)

2. Which is **not** the prime factorization for the number 42? (*Circle the correct letter.*)

A. 7 x 2 x 3   **C.** 2 x 7 x 3

B. 3 x 2 x 7   **D.** 2 x 7 x 2

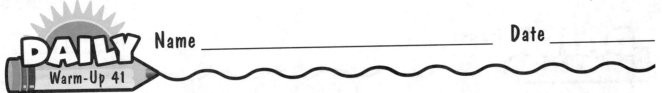

1. Mrs. Frankum buys apples by the basket. A small basket holds 18 apples and costs $10.50. A medium-sized basket holds 32 apples and costs $12.99. The largest basket holds 48 apples and costs $18.79. If Mrs. Frankum bought 3 small, 2 medium, and 5 large baskets, how many total apples did Mrs. Frankum buy? What would be the total cost? (*Show your work and circle your final answers.*)

2. Mrs. Hinojosa makes jelly each month to sell at a store. Each small batch of jelly will make 24 jars. Each large batch will make 48 jars. Yesterday, Mrs. Hinojosa made 192 jars of strawberry jelly. Which statement below is true about the number of batches of jelly Mrs. Hinojosa made yesterday? (*Circle the correct letter.*)

A. She made 3 large batches of jelly and 5 small batches of jellly.

B. She made 5 large batches of jelly and 2 small batches of jelly.

C. She made 3 large batches of jelly and 3 small batches of jelly.

D. She made 3 large batches of jelly and 2 small batches of jelly.

1. Michael drives a truck for a living. He drives Monday through Friday, driving an average of 9 hours each day. He drives 70 miles per hour. At this rate, how many miles will Michael drive in a 5-day period? (*Show your work and circle your final answer.*)

2. Pete went shopping for school clothes. He bought 5 shirts for $15.99 each, 3 packages of socks for $5 each, 4 pair of jeans for $45.94 each, and a pair of shoes for $54. Which expression shows how much money Pete spent altogether (not including tax)? (*Circle the correct letter.*)

A. (3 x $15.99) + (5 x $5) + (4 x $45.94) + $54 = ☐

B. (5 x $15.99) + (3 x $5) + (3 x $45.94) + $54 = ☐

C. (5 x $15.99) + (3 x $5) + (4 x $45.94) + $54 = ☐

D. (2 x $15.99) + (3 x $5) + (4 x $45.94) + $54 = ☐

Name _____ **Date** _____

DAILY
Warm-Up 43

1. Mary bought 3 teddy bears. She spent a total of $84.50. Which 3 bears did Mary buy? (*Circle the correct letter.*)

A. Penny, Peaches, and Sammy

B. Kyle, Penny, and Sammy

C. Peaches, Kyle, and Penny

D. Sammy, Peaches, and Kyle

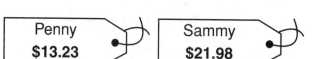

| Kyle $23.90 | Peaches $49.29 |
| Penny $13.23 | Sammy $21.98 |

2. Find the prime factorization for the number 480 using exponents. (*Show your work and circle your final answer.*)

Name _____ **Date** _____

DAILY
Warm-Up 44

1. Look at the display on the calculator. If the number on the display is the divisor and 259 is the quotient, which number below is the dividend? (*Circle the correct letter.*)

A. 21,749

B. 21,947

C. 21,479

D. 21,497

2. Solve the multiplication problems below.

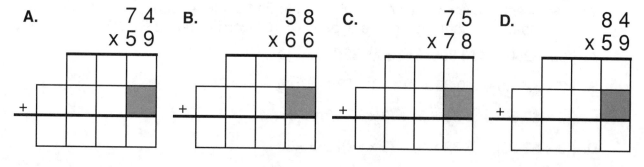

A. 7 4
    x 5 9

B. 5 8
    x 6 6

C. 7 5
    x 7 8

D. 8 4
    x 5 9

Name _____ **Date** _____

Warm-Up 45

1. Fill in the missing numbers to make the problem true.

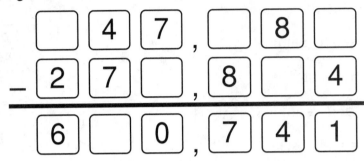

2. Fill in the boxes with your own numbers. Then multiply to find your answer.

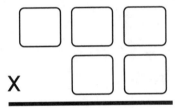

Name _____ **Date** _____

Warm-Up 46

1. Billy is a farmer. He is harvesting a field of rice that is 140 acres. Each day, he can harvest 35 acres of rice. How many days will it take Billy to harvest the entire field? (*Show your work and circle your final answer.*)

2. At a book store, Margo and her 2 friends bought 3 packages of batteries for $2.50 each, 3 bags of chips for $.89 each, and 3 bottles of water for $2 each. If they decide to split the cost evenly, which equation can be used to find *c*, the amount of money each person will need to pay for their part of the expense? (*Circle the correct letter.*)

A. [(3 x $250) + ($0.89 x 3) + (3 x $2)] ÷ 3 = *c*

B. [(3 x $2.50) + ($0.89 + 3) + (3 x $2)] ÷ 3 = *c*

C. [(3 x $2.50) + ($.89 x 3) + (3 x $2.50)] ÷ 3 = *c*

D. [(3 x $2.50) + ($.89 x 3) + (3 x $2)] ÷ 3 = *c*

Name _____ **Date** _____

Warm-Up 47

1. Fifteen adults decided to pool their money to buy paintings at an auction. On Monday, they bought 9 paintings for $279 each; on Tuesday, they bought 2 paintings for $789 each; and on Saturday, they bought 1 painting for $489. How much does each adult have to pay if they split the cost evenly? (*Circle the correct letter.*)

    A. $367.40   **B.** $276.00   **C.** $220.00   **D.** $305.20

2. Robert and his sister are buying kitchen supplies for the apartment they are sharing. They bought 6 plates for $1.50 each, 6 drinking glasses for $3.79 each, and 6 kitchen towels for $1.75 each. If Robert and his sister plan to share the cost evenly, how much will each person need to pay? (*Show your work and circle your final answer.*)

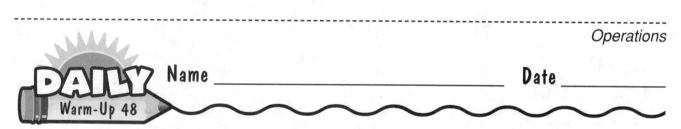

Name _____ **Date** _____

Warm-Up 48

1. Jennifer has 3 female Collies named Lola, Cindy, and Samantha. Last year, Cindy had 2 litters of puppies with 4 puppies in the first litter and 5 puppies in the second litter. Lola had 3 litters of puppies with 6 puppies in the first litter and 8 puppies in the second and third litters. Samantha had 2 litters of puppies with 3 puppies in the first litter and 6 puppies in the second litter. All of Lola's puppies sold for $125 each. All of Cindy's puppies sold for $200 each. All of Samantha's puppies sold for $375 each. How much total money did Jennifer make selling the puppies? (*Show your work and circle your final answer.*)

2. If you take the product of 38 and 42, then divide by 42, and then subtract 38, what would be the answer? (*Show your work and circle your final answer.*)

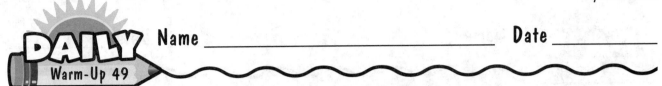

Name _____ **Date** _____

1. Sarah bought 2 boxes of pencils. There were 58 pencils in each box. In the first box, 23 of the pencils were red, 18 were blue, and the rest were yellow. In the second box, 16 were orange, 24 were blue, and the rest were yellow. How many total pencils in the boxes were yellow? (*Show your work and circle your final answer.*)

2. Thirty members of the school band were chosen to participate in a state contest. 20% of those band members were awarded individual ribbons at the contest. How many total band members were awarded individual ribbons? (*Show your work and circle your final answer.*)

Name _____ **Date** _____

1. Payton went to the bookstore to find historical books on the American Revolution. He bought 3 books for $12 each and 3 maps for $8 each. Which expression represents the total cost of Payton's purchase? (*Circle the correct letter.*)

A. (3 x $12) x (3 + $8)   **C.** (3 x $12) + (3 x $8)

B. (3 x $12) x (3 x $8)   **D.** (3 + $12) + (3 + $8)

2. Jimmy wants to purchase a new 27" TV. At TV Haven, a 27" TV is priced at $350. Since TV Haven is having a special, the TV is marked at $\frac{1}{4}$ off of the retail price minus a $50 mail-in-rebate. At Mann's TV, the same 27" TV is priced at $450. Mann's TV is also having a sale and is marking the TV at $\frac{1}{2}$ off of the suggested retail price. If Jimmy is looking for the best deal, where should he purchase his TV? (*Show your work and circle your final answer.*)

1. Mrs. Gold filled the tank in her truck with gasoline. She put 25 gallons of gas in the tank at the cost of $2.16 per gallon. If Mrs. Gold paid the cashier with $100, how much money did she get back? (*Show your work and circle your final answer.*)

2. Heath works at Scott's Deli from 6 A.M. to 11 A.M. every day and from 2 P.M. to 9 P.M. at Carry-Out Groceries every day. At Scott's Deli, Heath earns $6.50 per hour, and at Carry-Out Groceries he earns $8.20 per hour. If Heath works exactly the same hours each week, how much money will Heath make from both jobs in 4 weeks before taxes are taken out? (*Circle the correct letter.*)

A. $3,100.20

C. $2,607.20

B. $2,271.50

D. $2,517.20

---

1. Hank solved one of the problems below and got a correct quotient of 130. Which problem did Hank solve? (*Circle the correct letter.*)

A. 1560 ÷ 15 =   **B.** 1560 ÷ 14 =   **C.** 1560 ÷ 13 =   **D.** 1560 ÷ 12 =

2. Mrs. Kallina ordered 23 boxes of green pencils, 17 boxes of yellow pencils, 12 boxes of orange pencils, and 30 boxes of blue pencils for the new school year. In each box, there were 144 pencils. When the year was over, Mrs. Kallina took inventory and found she only had 17 boxes of green pencils, 12 boxes of yellow pencils, 5 boxes of orange pencils, and she was completely out of blue pencils. How many total pencils were used during the year? (*Show your work and circle your final answer.*)

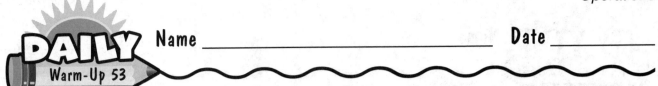

Name _____ Date _____

1. Brandi keeps $6 worth of quarters in a jar for every $10 worth of nickels in her piggy bank. If Brandi has $80 worth of nickels in her piggy bank, how much money in quarters does she have in the jar? (*Show your work and circle your final answer.*)

2. Lynn is looking at a pair of tennis shoes marked at $75. The store she is shopping at has a 60% off sale on every item in the store. If Lynn purchases the tennis shoes, how much will she pay (not including tax)? (*Circle the correct letter.*)

A. $40 **B.** $30 **C.** $50 **D.** $45

Name _____ Date _____

1. Which division problem below has a remainder? (*Circle the correct letter.*)

A. 1875 ÷ 15 **C.** 1862 ÷ 19

B. 1044 ÷ 18 **D.** 1380 ÷ 21

2. John's teacher asked him to come to the board and show the prime factorization for the number 36. Which answer choice is an **incorrect** answer for John to give? (*Circle the correct letter.*)

A. 3 x 2 x 2 x 3

B. 3 x 3 x 2 x 2

C. 2 x 3 x 2 x 3

D. 2 x 2 x 2 x 3

Name _____ **Date** _____

Warm-Up 55

1. Robin and Deron have a large spa in their backyard. The spa holds 800 gallons of water. For every 20 gallons of water, Robin and Deron must add $\frac{1}{4}$ of a cup of chlorine to the water. How many cups of chlorine must be added to the 800 gallons of water in the spa? (*Show your work and circle your final answer.*)

2. What should be done to write the fraction $\frac{3}{4}$ as a decimal?

   Explain:_____

   _____

   _____

- -

Name _____ **Date** _____

Warm-Up 56

1. Jimmy worked the problem below. How can Jimmy check his work? (*Circle the correct letter.*)

   A. Multiply the quotient by the dividend.

   B. Multiply the dividend by the divisor.

   C. Multiply the quotient by the divisor.

   D. This problem cannot be checked.

$$26\overline{)3250}^{\,125}$$

2. Cory gave Gordon half of his baseball cards. Gordon gave Brandy half of the baseball cards he received from Cory. Brandy kept 12 baseball cards and gave the remaining 6 to Mary. Mary kept half of the baseball cards and gave the remaining cards to Tim. How many baseball cards did Cory have in he beginning? (*Show your work and circle your final answer.*)

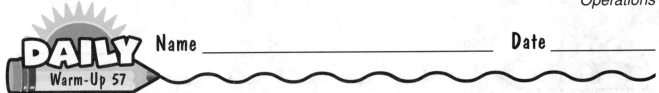

DAILY
Warm-Up 57

Name _____   Date _____

1. Mr. Acosta is teaching a lesson on bar graphs to his class. The 32 students in Mr. Acosta's class are asking 20 people who their favorite football team is. How many total people will be asked who their favorite football team is? (*Show your work and circle your final answer.*)

2. Mrs. Watkins does art projects with her students each Friday. All of the students in her class are making posters. Some of the posters were made from yellow construction paper and some of the posters were made from white construction paper. If there are 25 students in her class and two-fifths of them made their posters from white construction paper, how many students used yellow construction paper for their posters? (*Show your work and circle your final answer.*)

- -

DAILY
Warm-Up 58

Name _____   Date _____

1. Chris bought a large box of cheese for sandwiches. Each morning, he made 2 sandwiches for each of his 4 children. Chris used 2 pieces of cheese on each sandwich. If he did this each day during a 5-day school week, how many pieces of cheese did Chris use in a 10-day period? (*Show your work and circle your final answer.*)

2. Look at the problems below. Tyra worked one of the problems below and got a product of 11,214. Which problem did Tyra work? (*Circle the correct letter.*)

A. 7 2 5   B. 2 8 4   C. 1 7 8   D. 2 9 8
    x 5 9   x 9 3   x 6 3   x 9 7

16525
+3625 0
42,775

DAILY Warm-Up 59

Name _____ Date _____

1. Mrs. Savage is buying pencils to put in a container for her students. A package of pencils contains 8 pencils and costs $1.89. The container has the capacity to hold 90 pencils. How many packages of pencils must Mrs. Savage buy in order to fill the container as much as possible? (*Circle the correct letter.*)

   A. 9 packages   **B.** 10 packages   **C.** 11 packages   **D.** 12 packages

2. Coach Parson is trying to raise money for new gym equipment. New basketball equipment will cost $1,200, new soccer equipment will cost $899.35, and new equipment for the playground will cost $13,493.84. Coach Parson raised $7,492.02 more than he needed. How much money did Coach Parson raise altogether? (*Show your work and circle your final answer.*)

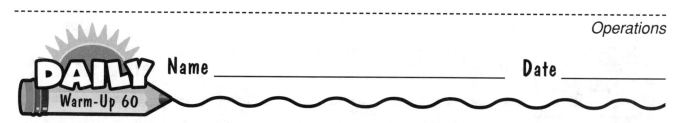

DAILY Warm-Up 60

Name _____ Date _____

1. Mike bought a new car stereo on sale. The price was 30% off of the retail price of the stereo. The stereo Mike bought had a retail price of $175. If Mike paid the cashier $200, how much money did he receive back? (*Show your work and circle your final answer.*)

2. When the students of Mr. Payne came into the class, the fractions below were written on the board. Students were asked to find which fraction was the largest. Mr. Payne asked Jimmy, a student in the class, to come to the board and circle the larger fraction. If Jimmy did this correctly, what fraction did he circle?

$$\frac{12}{15} \qquad\qquad \frac{5}{6}$$

Name _____ **Date** _____

Warm-Up 61

1. Cassidy wrote the math problem below for Joy to work. If Joy worked the problem correctly, which answer did Joy choose? (*Circle the correct letter.*)

> Which answer below is not a common multiple of 3 and 9?

A. 18 **B.** 27 **C.** 36 **D.** 39

2. Robin won 168 stuffed animals at the fair. She gave $\frac{1}{2}$ of them to her best friend. She then gave $\frac{1}{2}$ of the remaining stuffed animals to her cousin. How many stuffed animals does Robin have left? (*Show your work and circle your final answer.*)

- -

Name _____ **Date** _____

Warm-Up 62

1. Mrs. Woolf is doing many art projects with her students throughout the year. She has 22 students that each needs 21 sheets of orange construction paper, 14 sheets of yellow construction paper, 32 sheets of black construction paper, and 69 sheets of blue construction paper. Each package of construction paper holds 510 sheets of paper. Which statement about the number of packages of construction paper that Mrs. Woolf needs to order is **true**? (*Circle the correct letter.*)

   A. She needs to order 1 package of orange, 1 package of yellow, 2 packages of black, and 3 packages of blue construction paper.

   B. She needs to order 1 package of orange, 2 packages, of yellow, 1 package of black, and 1 package of blue construction paper.

   C. She needs to order 1 package of orange, 1 package of yellow, 2 packages of black, and 2 packages of blue construction paper.

   D. She needs to order 1 package of orange, 2 packages of yellow, 1 package of black, and 2 packages of blue construction paper.

2. If you multiply 15 and 38 then divide the product by 38, what quotient should you get? (*Circle the correct letter.*)

   A. 12 **B.** 13 **C.** 14 **D.** 15

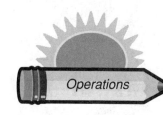

Answer Key

Warm-Up 1
1. 12 packages
2. 1,476 washing machines

Warm-Up 2
1. 1, 2, 4, 8; 8
2. B

Warm-Up 3
1. $2^3 \times 3^2$
2.

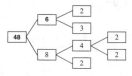

Warm-Up 4
1. Greatest: $\dfrac{5}{6}$

   Least: $\dfrac{5}{12}$
2. Chandler

Warm-Up 5
1. D
2. D

Warm-Up 6
1. D
2. 917 more cans

Warm-Up 7
1. D
2. $322.50

Warm-Up 8
1. A. 715,716
   B. 508,400
   C. 244,494
2. C

Warm-Up 9
1. $1,875
2. 770 students

Warm-Up 10
1. $2 \times 2 \times 2 \times 2 \times 5 \times 5$
2. $800

Warm-Up 11
1. 7,560 boxes
2. D

Warm-Up 12
1. D
2. 800 people

Warm-Up 13
1. C
2. $3^2 = 3 \times 3$; $4^2 = 4 \times 4$; $6^2 = 9 \times 4$

Warm-Up 14
1. $47.50
2. 9 more questions

Warm-Up 15
1. A. $\dfrac{3}{16}$

   B. $\dfrac{4}{9}$

   C. $\dfrac{11}{18}$

   D. $\dfrac{1}{14}$

   E. $\dfrac{7}{10}$

   F. $\dfrac{1}{2}$
2. $3^2 \times 7$

Warm-Up 16
1. Step 3; $184 \div 8 = 23$, not 24
2. D

Warm-Up 17
1. yes; 1,960
2. 9

Warm-Up 18
1. 30 cookies
2. D

Warm-Up 19
1. 65
2. 4,050 packages

Warm-Up 20
1. Hannah's dog: 40 lbs.
   Sarah's dog: 20 lbs.
2. 624 ounces; 39 pounds

Warm-Up 21
1. $4,694
2. A. 2,520 jars
   B. price per jar

Warm-Up 22
1. 85 boxes
2. 4,440 cookies were sold at the bake sale. 380 bags of cookies were left over.

Warm-Up 23
1. 33 dresses
2. 7 party favors

Warm-Up 24
1. $694.50
2. $812

Warm-Up 25
1. 2 students
2. $171.99

Warm-Up 26
1. C
2. 5,226.29

Warm-Up 27
1. 42
2. C

Warm-Up 28
1. $4,384
2. 30 pencils

Warm-Up 29
1. 34 yards
2. A. 94,710
   B. 444,066
   C. 255,192

Warm-Up 30
1. 45 cheerleaders
2. $178.85;

	Check #523
Corrina Jenson 3333 East Lane Victoria, MI 77482	
Pay to the Order of *Reddy's World*	$ 178.85
One hundred seventy-eight and 85 cents	
(Z) Zebra Banking 10209, South TX	*Corrina Jenson* Signature

Operations

Answer Key

Warm-Up 31
1. 50 students
2. A. 22
   B. 24
   C. 23

Warm-Up 32
1. 2 x 2 x 2 x 2 x 5 x 5
2. $3,132

Warm-Up 33
1. D
2. C

Warm-Up 34
1. A. 418,877
   B. 36
   C. 848,859
   D. 372,348
2. 375 students

Warm-Up 35
1. $5,625
2. $\frac{5}{10}$ or $\frac{1}{2}$

Warm-Up 36
1. $12,750
2. 39 points

Warm-Up 37
1. C
2. 18 months

Warm-Up 38
1. 100
2. No. 80% of 500 is 400, so they will be 40 lollipops short.

Warm-Up 39
1. 1,496 people
2. B

Warm-Up 40
1. $15.30
2. D

Warm-Up 41
1. 358 apples; $151.43
2. D

Warm-Up 42
1. 3,150 miles
2. C

Warm-Up 43
1. A
2. 2^5 x 3 x 5

Warm-Up 44
1. D
2. A. 4,366
   B. 3,828
   C. 5,850
   D. 4,956

Warm-Up 45
1. 947,585
   − 276,844
   ‾‾‾‾‾‾‾‾
    670,741
2. Answers will vary.

Warm-Up 46
1. 4 days
2. D

Warm-Up 47
1. D
2. $21.12

Warm-Up 48
1. $7,925
2. 0

Warm-Up 49
1. 35 yellow pencils
2. 6 band members

Warm-Up 50
1. C
2. TV Haven

Warm-Up 51
1. $46
2. D

Warm-Up 52
1. D
2. 6,912 pencils

Warm-Up 53
1. $48
2. B

Warm-Up 54
1. D
2. D

Warm-Up 55
1. 10 cups
2. Divide the numerator by the denominator to get 0.75.

Warm-Up 56
1. C
2. Cory had 72 cards.

Warm-Up 57
1. 640 people
2. 15 students

Warm-Up 58
1. 160 pieces of cheese
2. C

Warm-Up 59
1. C
2. $23,085.21

Warm-Up 60
1. $77.50
2. $\frac{5}{6}$

Warm-Up 61
1. D
2. 42 stuffed animals

Warm-Up 62
1. A
2. D

MEASUREMENT AND GEOMETRY

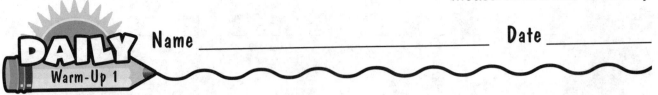

Name _____ **Date** _____

1. Which statement about a parallelogram is **not** correct? (*Circle the correct letter.*)

    A. Each set of opposite angles is congruent.

    B. Each set of opposite sides is congruent.

    C. Each set of opposite sides is parallel.

    D. All angles, when added together, equal 90°.

2. Label circumference, diameter, and radius on the model below.

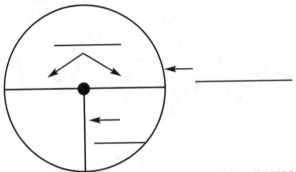

- -

Name _____ **Date** _____

1. Jeff drew the triangle below on the board. He gave the measure of one angle but asked his friend to find the measure of each of the two remaining angles. Which correct response did Jeff's friend give? (*Circle the correct letter.*)

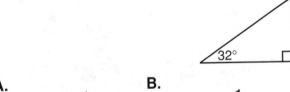

  A. 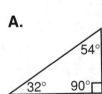   **B.** 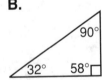   **C.** 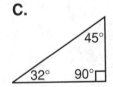   **D.**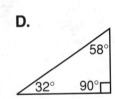

2. Jeff wrote the measures below for another triangle. He challenged his friend to find the correct angle measures for this new triangle. Which of the following could be the answer? (*Circle the correct letter.*)

    A. 110°, 67°, 54°   **C.** 90°, 45°, 60°

    B. 40°, 90°, 50°   **D.** 110°, 90°, 60°

Name _____ **Date** _____

1. Every summer, Terri mixes a combination of fertilizer and Wonder Grow to put on her rectangular yard. The yard measures 120 feet by 160 feet. Each combination she mixes will cover exactly 600 square feet. How many mixtures of fertilizer/Wonder Grow will Terri have to make? (*Show your work and circle your final answer.*)

2. Lee used 80 feet of fishing line from a spool that held 360 feet. How many **inches** of fishing line were left on the spool? (*Show your work and circle your final answer.*)

- -

Name _____ **Date** _____

1. Daniel made a swing for his children. From the swing he hung a tire. The tire had a radius of 8 inches. What can Daniel do to find the circumference of the tire? (*Circle the correct letter.*)

A. multiply π by 3.14

C. multiply π by 4

B. multiply 8 by π

D. multiply 8 x 2 x π

2. Which formula below will **not** give the circumference of the circle? (*Circle the correct letter.*)

A. C = π • 6 • 2   **C.** C = 12 • π

B. C = 2 • π • 6   **D.** C = π • 6

6 inches

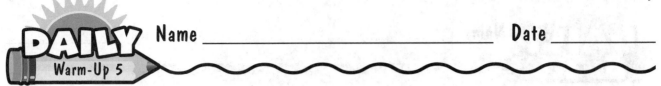

DAILY **Name** _____ **Date** _____
Warm-Up 5

1. What are the measures for angles *W*, *Y*, and *Z*? (*Circle the correct letter.*)

    A. *W* = 120° *Y* = 120° *Z* = 60°

    B. *W* =120° *Y* = 60°   *Z* = 120°

    C. *W* = 110° *Y* = 60°   *Z* = 170°

    D. *W* = 60°   *Y* = 120° *Z* = 120°

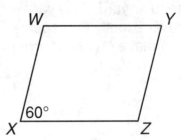

2. Look at the isosceles triangle below. The length of side *MN* is equal to the length of side *NO*. If ∠*M* = 55°, what is the measure of ∠*N*? (*Show your work and circle your final answer.*)

DAILY **Name** _____ **Date** _____
Warm-Up 6

1. Mary used 85 centimeters of lace on each of the 10 pillows she was making for her couch. What is the total amount of lace Mary used in **meters**? (*Show your work and circle your final answer.*)

2. Matt has two large dogs. The larger dog eats 3 pounds of dog food each day, and the smaller dog eats 2 pounds of dog food each day. How many **ounces** of dog food do both dogs eat in a 4-day period altogether? (*Show your work and circle your final answer.*)

Name _____   **Date** _____

Warm-Up 7

1. Jeffrey's toy got stuck on top of the shed in his backyard. The distance is 180 inches from the ground to the top of the shed. Calculate this distance in **feet**. (*Show your work and circle your final answer.*)

2. Abigail studied her math facts for 56 minutes on Monday. On Tuesday, she studied her math facts for 48 minutes. On Wednesday, she studied her math facts for 20 minutes more than she did on Monday. Thursday, she spent 19 fewer minutes studying her math facts than she did on Tuesday. What is the total amount of time Abigail spent studying her math facts altogether? (*Show your work and circle your final answer.*)

Name _____   **Date** _____

Warm-Up 8

1. Kurt and Leon were playing football. When Leon threw a pass to Kurt, the football landed 75 centimeters to the left of Kurt. How many **meters** to the left did the football land from Kurt? (*Circle the correct letter.*)

A. 75 meters   **B.** 0.75 meters   **C.** 7.5 meters   **D.** 0.075 meters

2. Look at the isosceles triangle Cherish drew on the board. How many lines of symmetry does the isosceles triangle have? Draw all lines of symmetry.

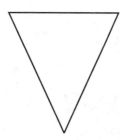

Name _____ **Date** _____

DAILY
Warm-Up 9

1. Ralph spends a lot of money on pool sticks. He keeps his pool sticks in a cabinet that is 4 ft. wide, 3 ft. deep, and 6 ft. high. What is the volume of the cabinet? (*Show your work and circle your final answer.*)

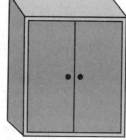

2. Which statement is **true** about a ray? (*Circle the correct letter.*)

   A. A line runs parallel with a ray at all times.

   B. A ray goes in one direction without an endpoint established.

   C. A ray has a beginning point and continues without an end.

   D. A ray continues in two directions without an end.

Name _____ **Date** _____

DAILY
Warm-Up 10

1. Cindy drew a square that has a perimeter of 10 meters. What is the length of each side? (*Show your work and circle your final answer.*)

2. Leeann drew the circle below on the board. The circle she drew has a diameter of 1 inch. What is the circumference of the circle? (*Show your work and circle your final answer.*)

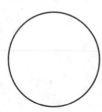

Name _____ **Date** _____

Warm-Up 11

1. Answer the questions about the shape Dominic drew on the board.

A. What is the area of the unshaded region?

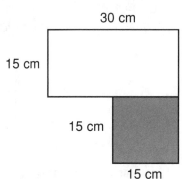

30 cm

15 cm

15 cm

15 cm

_____

B. What is the area of the shaded region?

_____

C. What is the combined area of the 2 shapes?

_____

2. What is the area of the triangle below?
(*Circle the correct letter.*)

A. 11 cm^2　　**B.** 24 cm^2

C. 20 cm^2　　**D.** 12 cm^2

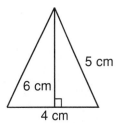

5 cm

6 cm

4 cm

Name _____ **Date** _____

Warm-Up 12

1. Which ruler shows the arrows pointing to the measurements $2\frac{3}{16}$, $2\frac{9}{16}$, $3\frac{3}{16}$, and $3\frac{12}{16}$?
(*Circle the correct letter.*)

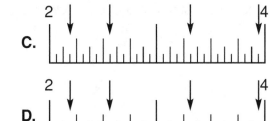

A.　3　　　　　　5

B.　2　　　　　　4

C.　2　　　　　　4

D.　2　　　　　　4

2. Courtney drew a square with a perimeter of 2.4 meters. What could Courtney do to find the length of each side? If she does this correctly, what answer will she get?

Explain:_____

_____

_____

Name _____ **Date** _____

1. Cody is mowing his grandma's yard. The shaded region in the model represents how much of the yard Cody has mowed. What is the area of the yard Cody has already mowed? (*Show your work and circle your final answer.*)

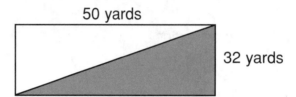

50 yards

32 yards

2. Look at the rectangular prism below. How many cubes were used to make the prism? (*Show your work and circle your final answer.*)

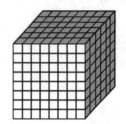

Name _____ **Date** _____

1. Terry is making dessert for her party. When shopping that morning, she bought 1 gallon of milk. The dessert she is making calls for a recipe of 1 pint of milk to be used for each pie she makes. Terry plans to make 4 pies. How many pints of milk will she have left? (*Show your work and circle your final answer.*)

2. What is the area of the parallelogram below? (*Show your work and circle your final answer.*)

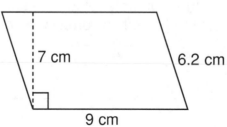

7 cm

6.2 cm

9 cm

Warm-Up 15

1. Mrs. Mann is teaching a geometry lesson to her students. She draws the shape below on the board. She asked her students to find the measure of angle *W* of the parallelogram. If her students answered correctly, what answer did they give? (*Circle the correct letter.*)

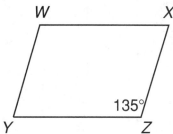

A. 45°

B. 135°

C. 180°

D. 145°

2. Agnes is sewing a blanket from pieces of scrap fabric. She cuts a circle with a circumference of 24 inches. What could be done to find the **diameter** of the circle Agnes cut for the blanket? (*Circle the correct letter.*)

A. add 24 + π   **C.** multiply 24 x π x 2

B. divide 24 by π   **D.** subtract 24 from π

Warm-Up 16

1. Which of the following could **not** be the measure of the angles of a triangle? (*Circle the correct letter.*)

A. 60° 90° 30°   **C.** 120° 30° 30°

B. 55° 75° 50°   **D.** 133° 90° 45°

2. What type of angle is angle *Y*? (*Circle the correct letter.*)

A. right   **C.** rotation

B. acute   **D.** obtuse

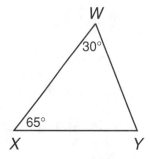

Name _____   **Date** _____

Warm-Up 17

1. Look at the isosceles triangle. The length of $\overline{AC}$ is equal to $\overline{CB}$. If m $\angle A = 65°$, what is m$\angle C$? (*Show your work and circle your final answer.*)

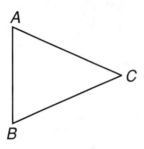

2. Liz is trying to name points on the number line. What points do A, B, C, and D represent?

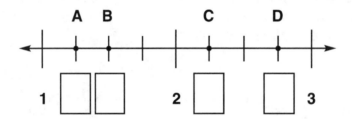

- -

Name _____   **Date** _____

Warm-Up 18

1. Sheryl is making a dessert for her son's engagement party. The recipe calls for two 8-ounce cans of strawberries. While shopping, Sheryl found frozen strawberries that came in a 1 pound, 7-ounce bag. How many ounces of strawberries will Sheryl have left if she buys the frozen strawberries? (*Show your work and circle your final answer.*)

2. Which two streets on the map below appear to be parallel? (*Circle the correct letter.*)

A. Allie Dr. and Beth Lane

B. Liz Blvd. and Allie Dr.

C. Liz Blvd. and Beth Lane

D. Jennifer St. and Beth Lane

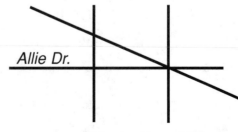

Name _____ **Date** _____

1. Which answer choice best describes ∠H?

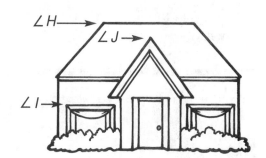

  A. right angle   **C.** obtuse angle

  B. bent angle   **D.** acute angle

2. Freddy needs supplies for a project at school. He bought 2 bottles of glitter for $0.96 each, 2 packages of construction paper for $1.87 each, 2 rulers for $1.93 each, and 2 large bottles of glue for $1.45 each. What is the best estimate of the amount of money Freddy spent on the supplies to the nearest dollar? (*Show your work and circle your final answer.*)

Name _____ **Date** _____

1. Sandra baby sits for extra money. She charges $10 for traveling and gas, plus $8 for each hour worked. To determine how much money she has earned, Sandra uses the equation $m = 10 + 8h$ to determine m, her earned money. If h represents the number of hours she baby sits, how much money will Sandra earn if she baby sits for 6 hours? (*Show your work and circle your final answer.*)

2. Heather drew the shape below on a piece of paper. She knows the measures of angles W and X. What statement is **true** about angles Y and Z? (*Circle the correct letter.*)

  A. Angle Y and Z equal angle W.

  B. Angle Y and Z each measure 180°.

  C. Angle Y and Z each measure 90°.

  D. Angle Y and Z each measure 360°.

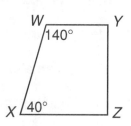

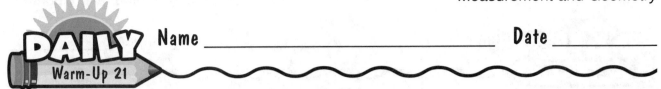

Name _____ **Date** _____

1. How long is the line segment to the nearest sixteenth of an inch? (*Circle your final answer.*)

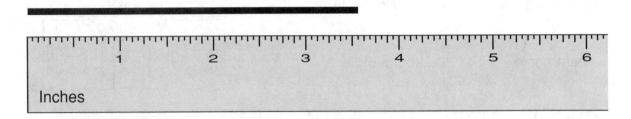

Inches

2. Janice multiplied five hundred eighteen times the number of ounces in two pounds. What product did Janice get? (*Show your work and circle your final answer.*)

Name _____ **Date** _____

1. Michael drew a rectangle that was 4 feet long and 10 feet wide. What is the area of the rectangle? What is the perimeter of the rectangle? (*Show your work and circle your final answers.*)

2. Which statement about the shape below is **not** true? (*Circle the correct letter.*)

A. Each pair of opposite sides is congruent.

B. Opposite sides are parallel.

C. Each angle is an acute angle.

D. The sum of all angles equal 360°.

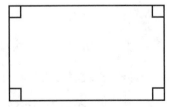

Name _____ **Date** _____

1. Christopher drew the triangle below on the board. Beside the triangle, he wrote the formula $A = \dfrac{b \times h}{2}$. If the base is 30 cm and the height is 10 cm, what is the area of the triangle? (*Show your work and circle your final answer.*)

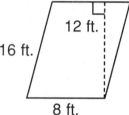

2. Find the perimeter and area of the parallelogram. (*Show your work and circle your final answers.*)

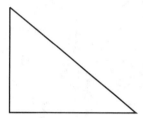

12 ft.

16 ft.

8 ft.

Name _____ **Date** _____

1. Heather is having a luncheon for her best friend. She bought 3 gallons of punch and wants to serve the punch in cups to her guests. If each guest drank exactly 1 cup and there was no punch left over, how many guests did Heather have at her party? (*Show your work and circle your final answer.*)

2. At Dawson Elementary, the Texas pledge is recited every morning during announcements. Look at the picture of the Texas flag. What type of angle is formed at each point of the star? (*Circle your final answer.*)

Name _____   **Date** _____

1. How long is the pencil to the nearest sixteenth of an inch? (*Circle your final answer.*)

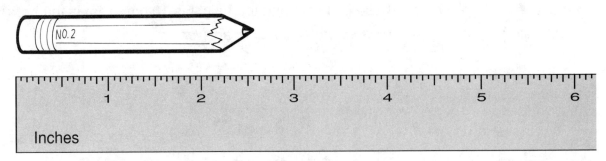

2. Cherish multiplied two hundred twelve times the number of ounces in a pound. What product did Cherish get? (*Show your work and circle your final answer.*)

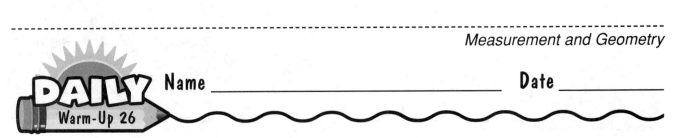

Name _____   **Date** _____

1. Use your ruler to draw a rectangle that is 3 cm wide and 8 cm long. What is the area of the rectangle? What is the perimeter? (*Show your work and circle your final answers.*)

2. Doug bought a new ice cooler for the fishing tournament he entered. The ice cooler has a capacity of 240 pounds. How many 10-pound catfish can Doug's cooler hold? (*Show your work and circle your final answer.*)

DAILY Warm-Up 27

1. Match the words with the correct definitions. Use the key as your guide.

_____ the distance from the center of a circle to a point on the circle

_____ a line segment that passes through the center point joining 2 points of the circle

_____ the perimeter of a circle

Key
A = Radius
B = Circumference
C = Diameter

2. What does the gray line segment represent in the picture below? (*Circle the correct letter.*)

A. center point   **C.** diameter

B. radius   **D.** circumference

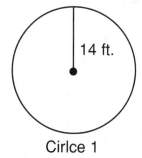

Name _____ Date _____

DAILY Warm-Up 28

1. Janet and Marissa each drank 5 glasses of milk from a 2-gallon jug. Each glass of milk held 2 cups. How much milk is left in the container? (*Show your work and circle your final answer.*)

2. Look at the two circles below. How much greater is the circumference of Circle 1 than the circumference of Circle 2? (*Show your work and circle your final answer.*)

14 ft.

Cirlce 1

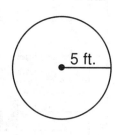

5 ft.

Circle 2

Name _____ **Date** _____

DAILY
Warm-Up 29

1. Six family members are taking an elevator to the 3rd floor of a shopping mall. The elevator has a capacity of 700 pounds. Two of the family members have a combined weight of 360 pounds, the next 2 family members have a combined weight of 420 pounds, and the last 2 have a combined weight of 160 pounds. If they obey the capacity of the elevator, how many trips will the elevator need to make to get all 6 family members to the 3rd floor? (*Show your work and circle your final answer.*)

2. Find the circumference of the circle below. (*Show your work and circle your final answer.*)

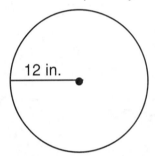

12 in.

Name _____ **Date** _____

DAILY
Warm-Up 30

1. Look at the figure below. The length of $\overline{AB}$ is 6 cm. The length of $\overline{AC}$ is 15 cm. What is the length of $\overline{BC}$? (*Circle your final answer.*)

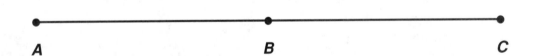

A   B   C

2. Use your pencil to draw a reflection of the figure shown on the grid.

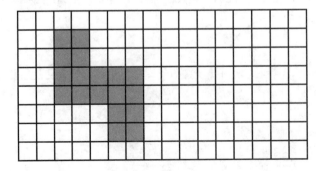

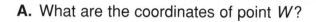

Name _____   **Date** _____

Warm-Up 31

1. Look at the coordinate grid to the right.

  A. What are the coordinates of point *W*?

  _____

  B. What point has the coordinates (2, 3)?

  _____

  C. What are the coordinates of point *Z*?

  _____

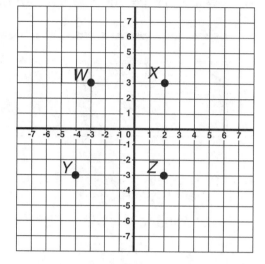

2. Tess wants to find how many months are in $\frac{3}{4}$ of a year. If she found the correct answer, what did she find? (*Show your work and circle your final answer.*)

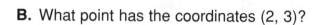

Name _____   **Date** _____

Warm-Up 32

1. The diameter of each wheel on a wagon is 4 feet. What is the circumference of each wheel? (*Show your work and circle your final answer.*)

2. Which expression shows how to find the circumference of the circle below? (*Circle the correct letter.*)

  A. (5 + 5) x π   **C.** 3.14 x π

  B. 5 x 3.14   **D.** (5 x 3) x 3.14

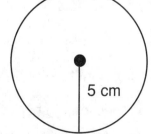

5 cm

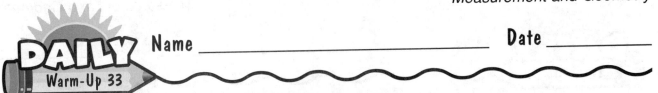

DAILY
Warm-Up 33

1. How long is the line segment to the nearest sixteenth-inch? (*Circle your final answer.*)

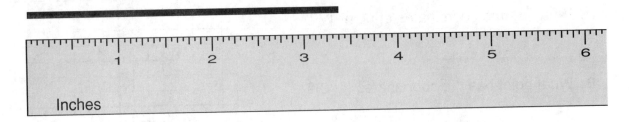

Inches

2. Jake drew the triangle below on a sheet of paper. Which of the following is true about the triangle Jake drew?

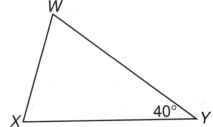

A. ∠W and ∠X = 140°

B. ∠Y and ∠X = 140°

C. ∠W and ∠Y = 140°

D. ∠W and ∠X and ∠Y = 140°

- -

DAILY
Warm-Up 34

1. Timothy has 2 dump trucks that carry a capacity of 3 tons each. If Timothy has 24,000 pounds of gravel he needs delivered to a customer, and he plans to use both dump trucks for the job, how many loads will each dump truck need to haul? (*Show your work and circle your final answer.*)

2. Look at the two shapes. Which statement is true? (*Circle the correct letter.*)

A. Both shapes have 2 sets of parallel lines.

B. Shape Y has more sets of parallel lines than shape Z.

C. Shape Y is congruent to shape Z.

D. Shape Y is a reflection of shape Z.

DAILY
Warm-Up 35

Name _____   Date _____

1. What is the perimeter of the rectangle below? (*Show your work and circle your final answer.*)

$1\frac{1}{8}$ inches

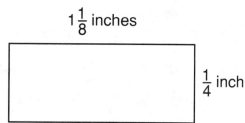

$\frac{1}{4}$ inch

2. Lee went fishing and caught 3 fish. The first fish weighed 3 pounds 4 ounces. The second fish weighed 8 ounces less than the first fish. The third fish weighed twice as much as the second fish. How much did the third fish weigh? (*Show your work and circle your final answer.*)

DAILY
Warm-Up 36

Name _____   Date _____

1. Look at the segments below. Which segment appears to be perpendicular to $\overline{NQ}$? (*Circle the correct letter.*)

A. $\overline{MQ}$

B. $\overline{OQ}$

C. $\overline{QP}$

D. $\overline{QO}$

N

M

O

Q

P

2. What time is 7 hours and 30 minutes after 8:30 A.M.? (*Circle your final answer.*)

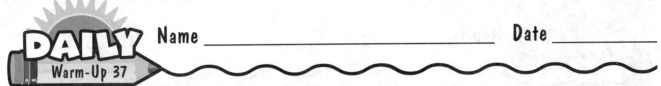

Name _____ **Date** _____

Warm-Up 37

1. Anna is putting lights on the roof of her house. The length of her house is 52 feet. She can purchase the lights in 6-foot, 12-foot, 16-foot, or 18-foot strands. If she wants just enough lights to go across the length of her house without any lights hanging over, which would be the smartest choice for Anna to make? (*Circle the correct letter.*)

   A. Purchase three 6-foot strands and one 16-foot strand.

   B. Purchase two 18-foot strands and one 16-foot strand.

   C. Purchase nine 6-foot strands.

   D. Purchase three 12-foot strands and one 18-foot strand.

2. Which of these shapes could never have parallel lines? (*Circle the correct letter.*)

   A. trapezoid   **B.** square   **C.** rectangle   **D.** circle

---

Name _____ **Date** _____

Warm-Up 38

1. If ∠*W* and ∠*X* of a parallelogram labeled *WXYZ* equal 140°, then ∠*Y* and ∠*Z* must equal _____? (*Show your work and circle your final answer.*)

2. Which statement about the figure below is **not** true? (*Circle the correct letter.*)

   A. The shape is a cone.

   B. The shape is a solid figure.

   C. The shape has one curved surface.

   D. The shape has three vertices.

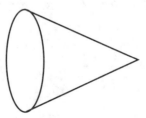

Name _____ Date _____

Warm-Up 39

1. Today is March 2nd. What day of the week
will it be in 25 days? (*Circle your final answer.*)

March						
SUNDAY	**MONDAY**	**TUESDAY**	**WEDNESDAY**	**THURSDAY**	**FRIDAY**	**SATURDAY**
		1	2	3	4	5
6	7	8	9	10	11	12
13	14	15	16	17	18	19
20	21	22	23	24	25	26
27	28	29	30	31		

2. Charles needs $2\frac{1}{2}$ gallons of punch for his sister's party. How many **pints** of punch does
Charles need? (*Show your work and circle your final answer.*)

Name _____ Date _____

Warm-Up 40

1. If the diameter of a circle is 6 feet, what would be the circumference of the circle? (*Show
your work and circle your final answer.*)

2. Jerry's dog Fetch retrieved a 36-inch stick when Jerry threw it. How many **feet** long is
the stick Jerry threw? (*Show your work and circle your final answer.*)

Name _____   **Date** _____

Warm-Up 41

1. Dale is planting a vegetable garden that measures 15 feet by 9 feet. What is the formula for finding the perimeter of the garden? (*Circle the correct letter.*)

A. $A = 2 \times (l + w)$ **C.** $A = \dfrac{b \times h}{2}$

B. $P = \dfrac{b \times h}{2}$ **D.** $P = 2 \times (l + w)$

2. When Lauren awoke at 7:00 A.M., the temperature was 43°F. By 3:00 P.M., the temperature was 17° warmer. What was the temperature at 3:00 P.M.? (*Show your work and circle your final answer.*)

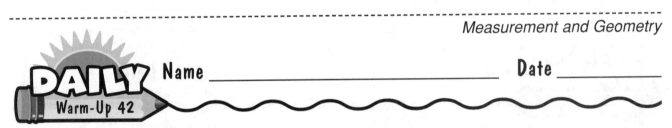

Name _____   **Date** _____

Warm-Up 42

1. Beth drew a square that had a perimeter of 60 centimeters. She asked John to write four statements about the square she drew. Which statement below that John made is **not** correct? (*Circle the correct letter.*)

A. The square has an area of 225 square centimeters.

B. The square has a perimeter of 60 centimeters.

C. The square has an area of 300 square centimeters.

D. Each side of the square has a length of 15 centimeters.

2. Which image shows a **reflection** of the letter? (*Circle the correct letter.*)

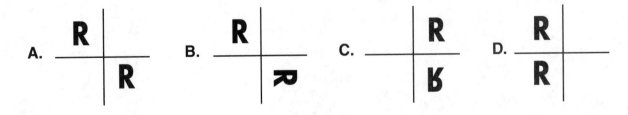

Name _____ Date _____

1. Brandy's bedroom is 9 feet long. The area of her bedroom is 54 square feet. What is the **perimeter** of Brandy's bedroom? (*Show your work and circle your final answer.*)

2. Jack is playing a card game. Whenever a person draws a card from the deck, that person must find the card's equivalent. The card Jack drew read "7,000 centimeters." Which card below must Jack choose to obtain the card's equivalent? (*Circle the correct letter.*)

A. | 700 millimeters |

C. | 70 meters |

B. | 70 kilometers |

D. | 7 yards |

Name _____ Date _____

1. When the students in Mrs. Rome's class entered the room, they had the following question on the overhead: What shape has no right angles but has four equal sides? (*Circle the correct letter.*)

A. square   **B.** rhombus   **C.** triangle   **D.** rectangle

2. Damon filled a 32-ounce plastic cup with cola. How many **cups** of cola is this? (*Show your work and circle your final answer.*)

DAILY
Warm-Up 45

Name _____   Date _____

1. Carol turned on the sprinkler in her yard. The sprinkler, after revolving in a complete circle, sprayed water at a radius of 6 feet. What is the **area** of the water circle? (*Show your work and circle your final answer.*)

2. Place the decimals and fractions below in their correct locations on the number line.

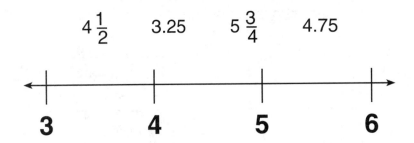

$$4\frac{1}{2} \qquad 3.25 \qquad 5\frac{3}{4} \qquad 4.75$$

3   **4**   **5**   **6**

DAILY
Warm-Up 46

Name _____   Date _____

1. Which formula can be used to find the number of edges each shape has? (*Circle the correct letter.*)

A. $E = V - F - 2$

B. $E = (5 + 5 - 2)$

C. $E = F + V + 2$

D. $E = V + F - 2$

Shape Name	# of Vertices (V)	# of Faces (F)	# of Edges (E)
Square prism	5	5	8
Rectangular pyramid	5	5	8
Rectangular prism	8	6	12
Cube	8	6	12

2. How many days are in January, March, July, September, and November altogether? (*Show your work and circle your final answer.*)

DAILY
Warm-Up 47

Name _____   Date _____

1. Which of the following shapes is the shape of a stop sign? (*Circle the correct letter.*)

   A. triangle   **B.** circle   **C.** hexagon   **D.** octagon

2. Which of the following shapes is the shape of a yield sign? (*Circle the correct letter.*)

   A. octagon   **B.** pentagon   **C.** triangle   **D.** parallelogram

----

DAILY
Warm-Up 48

Name _____   Date _____

1. Look at the model to the right. $\overline{UW}$ is congruent to _____ .

   A. $\overline{YV}$ **C.** $\overline{UV}$

   B. $\overline{VW}$ **D.** $\overline{WX}$

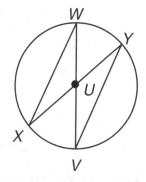

2. Name each shape and determine how many edges, vertices, and faces each shape has.

   A.

   Shape name: _____

   Number of vertices: _____

   Number of edges: _____

   Number of faces: _____

   B.

   Shape name: _____

   Number of vertices: _____

   Number of edges: _____

   Number of faces: _____

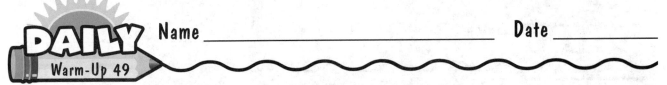

Name _____ **Date** _____

Warm-Up 49

1. Sam is making a small kennel for his dog Spot. He wants to put a fence around the kennel. The width of the kennel is 5 feet and the length of the kennel is 10 feet. He can buy the fencing in 6-foot, 8-foot, 10-foot, or 12-foot pieces. If Sam doesn't want any fencing left over, which would be the smartest buy for Sam to make? (*Circle the correct letter.*)

   A. Buy three 6-foot pieces of fencing.

   B. Buy three 8-foot pieces of fencing.

   C. Buy three 10-foot pieces of fencing.

   D. Buy three 12-foot pieces of fencing.

2. If you planned to find the weight of a truck, which unit of measurement would be the best? (*Circle the correct letter.*)

   A. ounces   **B.** tons   **C.** inches   **D.** liters

Name _____ **Date** _____

Warm-Up 50

1. Marsha is baking a cake from a recipe her grandmother gave to her. The recipe calls for a $\frac{1}{2}$ cup of sugar. Circle the fraction below that is less than $\frac{1}{2}$.

   $$\frac{3}{7} \qquad \frac{4}{5} \qquad \frac{4}{8} \qquad \frac{5}{7}$$

2. Write each shape name in the correct column below.

More Than 4 Vertices	Less Than 4 Vertices	No Vertices

Rectangular prism

Square pyramid

Cone

Triangular prism

Sphere

Cylinder

Name _____ Date _____

1. If there are 52 weeks in 1 year, how many **years** are in 416 weeks? (*Show your work and circle your final answer.*)

2. Which two shape names do not belong with the others? (*Circle your final answers.*)

triangular prism	cube	rectangular prism
cylinder	rectangle	cone
sphere	rectangular pyramid	hexagon

Name _____ Date _____

1. Use the key to find the missing word in the concept circle.

Key	
pound	quart
ounce	gram
ton	cup
milligram	yard

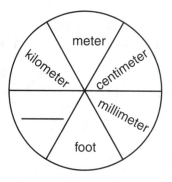

2. Look at the line segment. Use the clues below to find the length of $\overline{AD}$ in centimeters. (*Show your work and circle your final answer.*)

- $\overline{CD}$ is equal to $\overline{BC}$.
- $\overline{BC}$ is $\frac{1}{2}$ of the length of $\overline{AB}$.
- $\overline{AB}$ is 86 cm.

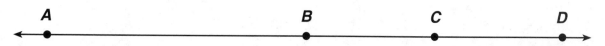

A   B   C   D

DAILY
Warm-Up 53

Name _____ Date _____

1. What shape would this make if it was cut out and folded? (*Circle your final answer.*)

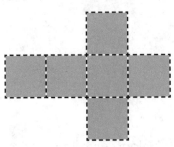

2. James is putting landscaping timber around two flower gardens that are in the shape of an octagon and hexagon. How many total feet of landscaping timber does James need to buy? (*Show your work and circle your final answer.*)

10 ft.

12 ft.

- -

Measurement and Geometry

DAILY
Warm-Up 54

Name _____ Date _____

1. Sally and David each drew a parallelogram on a sheet of paper. Which friend found the measurement of each angle correctly? (*Circle your final answer.*)

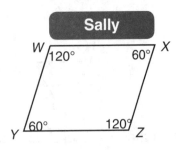

Sally

W 120°   60° X

Y 60°   120° Z

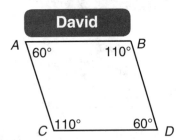

David

A 60°   110° B

C 110°   60° D

2. Mike used a sheet of blue construction paper to glue on his artwork. The length of each side of the construction paper was 14 inches. What is the area of the construction paper? (*Circle the correct letter.*)

A. 56 in.^{2} **C.** 336 in.^{2}

B. 28 in.^{2} **D.** 196 in.^{2}

102

1. Cassidy threw the football 28 yards on her first attempt, 48 yards on her second attempt, and 38 yards on her third attempt. How many total **feet** did Cassidy throw the football altogether? (*Show your work and circle your final answer.*)

2. Mrs. Hargrove has two identical pots she uses for cooking. Each pot weighs exactly 6 pounds. How many **ounces** do both pots weigh altogether? (*Show your work and circle your final answer.*)

---

1. Four friends were supposed to name a three-dimensional shape. Which shape is not three-dimensional? (*Circle the correct letter.*)

   A. cone   **B.** trapezoid   **C.** cylinder   **D.** cube

2. Which term identifies the solid black dot in the circle below? (*Circle the correct letter.*)

   A. circumference   **C.** diameter

   B. radius   **D.** center point

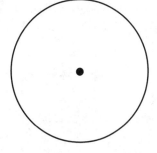

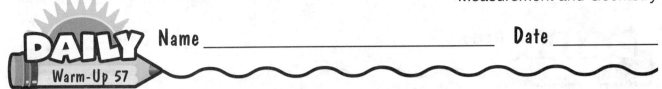

DAILY
Warm-Up 57

Name _____   Date _____

1. Kurt marked off a rectangular space on the gym floor. The rectangular space measured 19 by 20 meters. What is the area of the rectangle? (*Show your work and circle your final answer.*)

2. Jack has a rope that is 960 inches long. How long is the rope in **feet**? (*Show your work and circle your final answer.*)

DAILY
Warm-Up 58

Name _____   Date _____

1. Joy is making a circular garden out of landscaping timber. In the garden, she will plant yellow roses. The garden has a diameter of 12 feet. How many total feet of landscaping timber will Joy need? (*Show your work and circle your final answer.*)

2. It is winter, and a severe cold front has moved into the Gulf Coastal plains region. At 4:00 P.M., the temperature was a chilly 46°F. If the temperature falls 2° each hour, what will the temperature be at 8:00 P.M.? (*Show your work and circle your final answer.*)

Name _____ **Date** _____

Warm-Up 59

1. Tina drew two lines on a sheet of paper. She labeled the lines *W* and *Y*. The lines intersected to form a 90° angle. Which geometric term below describes the intersecting lines? (*Circle the correct letter.*)

   A. circumference   **C.** perpendicular

   B. diameter   **D.** horizontal

2. Draw three angles as mentioned below.

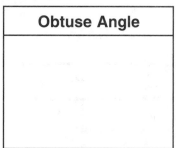

Acute Angle	Obtuse Angle	Right Angle

Name _____ **Date** _____

Warm-Up 60

1. Which is true about a rectangular prism? (*Circle the correct letter.*)

   A. A rectangular prism has 1 square face, 8 edges, 5 vertices, and 4 triangular faces.

   B. A rectangular prism has 8 square faces, 6 vertices, and 12 edges.

   C. A rectangular prism has the same number of faces, edges, and vertices as a cube.

   D. A rectangular prism has 1 curved face.

2. Use the key to solve the problems below.

   A. A _____ has 5 faces, 9 edges, and 6 vertices.

   B. A _____ has 6 faces, 8 vertices, and 12 edges.

   C. A _____ has 5 faces, 8 edges, and 5 vertices.

   D. A _____ has 1 vertex, 1 curved surface, and 1 circular base.

Key
W. cone
X. rectangular prism
Y. triangular prism
Z. square pyramid

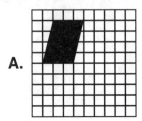 **DAILY**
Warm-Up 61

Name _____ **Date** _____

1. Which figure shows a rotation? (*Circle the correct letter.*)

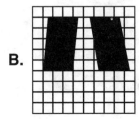 **A.**   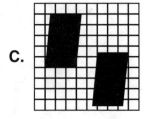 **B.**   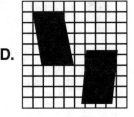 **C.**   **D.**

2. Use your ruler to measure the length of the paintbrush to the nearest inch. (*Circle your final answer.*)

 **DAILY**
Warm-Up 62

Name _____ **Date** _____

1. Mrs. Alvarado drew a triangle on the board. Taylor measured the 3 angles of the triangle. If the sum of the first 2 angles was 130°, what statement below will give her the measurement of the third angle? (*Circle the correct letter.*)

A. add 130° twice, and then subtract from 360°

B. subtract 130° from 180°

C. add 130° to 180°

D. subtract 130° from 360°

2. Which formula below will give the circumference of the circle?
(*Circle the correct letter.*)

A. $C = \pi \times 12$ **C.** $C = 12 \times 2$

B. $C = 12 \times \pi \times 2$ **D.** $C = 12 \times 12$

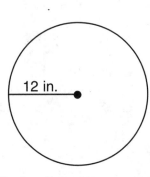

12 in.

Answer Key

Warm-Up 1
1. D
2.

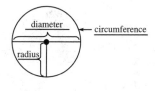

Warm-Up 2
1. D
2. B

Warm-Up 3
1. 32 mixtures
2. 3,360 inches

Warm-Up 4
1. D
2. D

Warm-Up 5
1. B
2. 70°

Warm-Up 6
1. 8.5 meters
2. 320 ounces

Warm-Up 7
1. 15 feet
2. 209 minutes

Warm-Up 8
1. B
2. 1; ▽

Warm-Up 9
1. 72 ft.^{3}
2. C

Warm-Up 10
1. 2.5 meters
2. 3.14 inches

Warm-Up 11
1. A. 450 cm^2
   B. 225 cm^2
   C. 675 cm^2
2. D

Warm-Up 12
1. B
2. Divide 2.4 by 4 to get the length. The length of each side will be 0.6 meters.

Warm-Up 13
1. 800 yards^2
2. 384 cubes

Warm-Up 14
1. 4 pints
2. 63 cm^2

Warm-Up 15
1. B
2. B

Warm-Up 16
1. D
2. B

Warm-Up 17
1. 50°
2. A: $1\frac{1}{4}$
   B: $1\frac{1}{2}$
   C: $2\frac{1}{4}$
   D: $2\frac{3}{4}$

Warm-Up 18
1. 7 ounces
2. C

Warm-Up 19
1. C
2. $12

Warm-Up 20
1. $58
2. C

Warm-Up 21
1. $3\frac{9}{16}$ inches
2. 16,576

Warm-Up 22
1. A = 40 feet^2; P = 28 feet
2. C

Warm-Up 23
1. 150 cm^2
2. Perimeter: 48 feet
   Area: 96 feet^2

Warm-up 24
1. 48 guests
2. acute

Warm-Up 25
1. $2\frac{9}{16}$ inches
2. 3,392

Warm-Up 26
1. Area: 24 cm^2
   Perimeter: 22 cm
2. 24 catfish

Warm-Up 27
1. A, C, B
2. C

Warm-Up 28
1. 12 cups of milk
2. 56.52 ft.

Warm-Up 29
1. 2 trips
2. 75.36 in.

Warm-Up 30
1. 9 cm
2.

Warm-Up 31
1. A. (-3, 3)
   B. X
   C. (2, -3)
2. 9 months

Warm-Up 32
1. 12.56 feet
2. A

Warm-Up 33
1. $3\frac{6}{16}$ inches
2. A

Answer Key

Warm-Up 34
1. 2 loads each
2. B

Warm-Up 35
1. $2\frac{3}{4}$ in. or 2.75 in.
2. 5 lbs. 8 oz. or 88 oz.

Warm-Up 36
1. C
2. 4:00 P.M.

Warm-Up 37
1. B
2. D

Warm-Up 38
1. 220°
2. D

Warm-Up 39
1. Sunday
2. 20 pints

Warm-Up 40
1. 18.84 feet
2. 3 feet

Warm-Up 41
1. D
2. 60°F

Warm-Up 42
1. C
2. C

Warm-Up 43
1. 30 feet
2. C

Warm-Up 44
1. B
2. 4 cups

Warm-Up 45
1. 113.04 feet^2
2.

Warm-Up 46
1. D
2. 153 days

Warm-Up 47
1. D
2. C

Warm-Up 48
1. C
2. A. rectangular prism
   vertices: 8
   edges: 12
   faces: 6
   B. square pyramid
   vertices: 5
   edges: 8
   faces: 5

Warm-Up 49
1. C
2. B

Warm-Up 50
1. $\frac{3}{7}$
2.

More Than 4 Vertices	Less Than 4 Vertices	No Vertices
• rectangular prism • square pyramid • triangular prism	• cone	• sphere • cylinder

Warm-Up 51
1. 8 years
2. hexagon and rectangle

Warm-Up 52
1. yard
2. 172 cm

Warm-Up 53
1. cube
2. 152 ft.

Warm-Up 54
1. Sally
2. D

Warm-Up 55
1. 342 feet
2. 192 ounces

Warm-Up 56
1. B
2. D

Warm-Up 57
1. 380 m^2
2. 80 feet

Warm-Up 58
1. 37.68 ft.
2. 38°F

Warm-Up 59
1. C
2. Answers may vary.

Warm-Up 60
1. C
2. A. Y
   B. X
   C. Z
   D. W

Warm-Up 61
1. A
2. 6 inches

Warm-Up 62
1. B
2. B

GRAPHS, DATA AND PROBABILITY

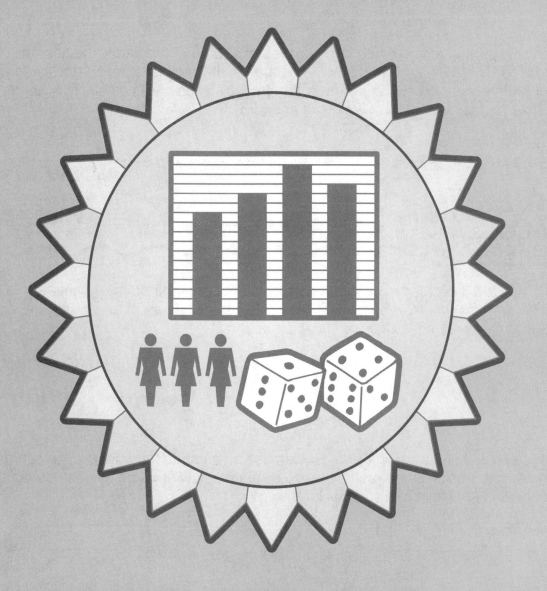

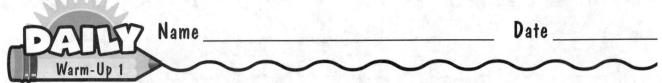

DAILY Warm-Up 1   Name _____   Date _____

1. Ernest is playing a board game with Calley that uses the spinner below. If the spinner is spun twice, which tree diagram shows all possible outcomes the pointer can land on during both spins? (*Circle the correct letter.*)

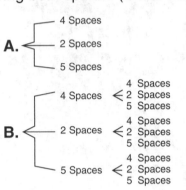

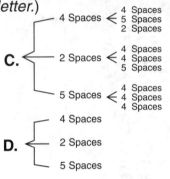

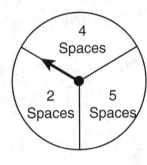

A.
— 4 Spaces
— 2 Spaces
— 5 Spaces

B.
4 Spaces < 4 Spaces / 2 Spaces / 5 Spaces
2 Spaces < 4 Spaces / 2 Spaces / 5 Spaces
5 Spaces < 4 Spaces / 2 Spaces / 5 Spaces

C.
4 Spaces < 4 Spaces / 5 Spaces / 2 Spaces
2 Spaces < 4 Spaces / 4 Spaces / 5 Spaces
5 Spaces < 4 Spaces / 4 Spaces / 4 Spaces

D.
— 4 Spaces
— 2 Spaces
— 5 Spaces

2. Cindy is playing a card game with her brother. Three of the cards she has are 7s, three other cards are 8s, and two of the cards are 9s. If Cindy lays the cards facedown, and her brother selects one card, what is the probability the card he selects is not an 8? (Show your work and circle your final answer.)

- -

DAILY Warm-Up 2   Name _____   Date _____

1. On Monday, Jared can wear either a pair of jeans or a pair of khaki pants with a blue, white, or red shirt. How many possible combinations of 1 pant and 1 shirt are possible? (*Show your work and circle your final answer.*)

2. Jefferson is doing an art project. He can use a paintbrush or sponge. He can use green, red, or blue paint. Complete the diagram below showing all possible combinations Jefferson can use in his art project.

DAILY Warm-Up 3

Name _____ Date _____

1. Daveon put a quarter in a gumball machine and received 2 green gumballs, 2 blue gumballs, and 2 red gumballs. Daveon placed these gumballs in a small bag. If he grabs 2 gumballs out of the bag without looking, how many color combinations are possible? (*Show your work and circle your final answer.*)

2. Frank, Peter, Bill, Sam, and Robert entered a race at the track meet. Bill, Peter, and Sam finished 1st, 2nd, or 3rd. How many possible ways could Bill, Peter, and Sam finish the race? (*Show your work and circle your final answer.*)

DAILY Warm-Up 4

Name _____ Date _____

1. Linda bought a package of hair ribbons. There were 9 blue ribbons, 4 yellow ribbons, 3 pink ribbons, and 2 orange ribbons in the package. If Linda grabs 1 hair ribbon without looking, what is the probability she will select a pink ribbon? (*Show your work and circle your final answer.*)

2. The grades below show what Heath scored on eight math assignments. What is the mode of his grades? (*Circle your final answer.*)

> 72, 84, 90, 84, 91, 68, 84, and 78

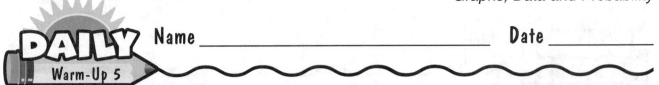

DAILY Warm-Up 5

Name _____ Date _____

1. The table below shows the number of newspapers Jason delivered on his paper route during a 7-day period. Which of the following measures of the data gives an answer of 104? (*Circle the correct letter.*)

Newspapers	93	99	102	93	193	89	129
Day	Mon.	Tue.	Wed.	Thur.	Fri.	Sat.	Sun.

A. Median **B.** Range **C.** Mean **D.** Mode

2. Mandy is eating cookies from a package she just bought. In the package, there are 6 chocolate cookies and 10 cinnamon cookies. If Mandy grabs 1 cookie without looking, what is the probability that the cookie she selects will be a chocolate cookie? (*Circle the correct letter.*)

A. $\frac{10}{6}$ **B.** $\frac{6}{10}$ **C.** $\frac{2}{8}$ **D.** $\frac{3}{8}$

DAILY Warm-Up 6

Name _____ Date _____

1. Michael needs to do a total of 3 chores on Monday, Tuesday, and Wednesday. He needs to wash his car, mow the lawn, and clean his room. He wants to do each chore on a different day. How many possible combinations of 1 chore per day can Michael get his chores done? (*Show your work and circle your final answer.*)

2. For making the honor roll at school, Audra's mother made cupcakes for her to eat after school. She made 2 chocolate cupcakes, 3 vanilla cupcakes, and 1 strawberry cupcake. If Audra grabbed 2 cupcakes without looking, list the possible combinations Audra could have grabbed.

Name _____   Date _____

1. Two contestants participating in a stunt are using the spinner below to determine which contestant will go first. Each contestant is hoping to land on a number greater than 5 so they can watch other contestants do their stunts and learn from their mistakes. If Cindy, a contestant, spins the spinner once, what is the probability she will land on a number greater than 5? (*Circle the correct letter.*)

A. $\frac{3}{8}$ **B.** $\frac{1}{2}$ **C.** $\frac{4}{8}$ **D.** $\frac{4}{8}$

2. Mary is making a blanket. She decides to sew different color buttons at random around the center of the blanket. She has 12 green buttons, 2 red buttons, 3 blue buttons, 5 orange buttons, and 2 yellow buttons in a jar. If Mary selects 1 button from the jar without looking, what is the probability that she will select a red button? (*Show your work and circle your final answer.*)

- -

Name _____   Date _____

1. Sara is choosing an outfit for a party she is attending. She can choose to wear a blue, white, red, or orange shirt. She can also choose to wear khaki or navy pants. How many possible combinations of 1 color shirt and 1 type of pants are there to choose from? (*Show your work and circle your final answer.*)

2. This morning, the weather forecast said the chance of rain is 60%. Does the forecast mean the chance of rain is likely or not likely?

Explain: _____

_____

_____

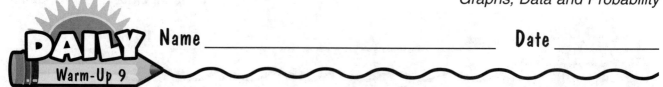

1. Jennifer has a standard deck of cards. There are 52 cards in the deck. If Jennifer selects 1 card from the deck without looking, what is the probability of Jennifer selecting a king? Reduce the fraction to lowest terms. (*Show your work and circle your final answer.*)

2. Jackson is in a race with three other people. What is the probability that Jackson will finish first? (*Show your work and circle your final answer.*)

- -

1. Isaac is taking measurements in the changes of temperature over a period of time. What type of graph should Isaac use to display his data? (*Circle the correct letter.*)

   A. pie chart   **B.** pictograph   **C.** line graph   **D.** circle graph

2. If the spinner below is spun once, what is the probability that it will land on the color blue? (*Circle the correct letter.*)

   A. 2 out of 9   **B.** 4 out of 9

   C. 2 out of 1   **D.** 1 out of 2

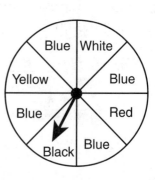

Name _____ Date _____

1. Maria has 24 quarters and 16 dimes in her purse. If she takes 1 coin from her purse without looking, what is the probability that the coin will be a quarter? (*Circle the correct letter.*)

   A. 2 out of 3

   B. 2 out of 3

   C. 3 out of 5

   D. 2 out of 5

2. Of the 36 prizes Isaac is searching for, 8 prizes have money hidden inside. What is the probability that Isaac will find a prize with money inside? (*Show your work and circle your final answer.*)

- -

Name _____ Date _____

1. Robert bought a box of colored toothpicks. There were 6 red toothpicks, 8 green toothpicks, 4 yellow toothpicks, and 6 blue toothpicks in the box. If Robert takes 1 toothpick from the box without looking, what is the probability that he will **not** pick a green toothpick? (*Circle the correct letter.*)

   A. 2 out of 3

   B. 1 out of 2

   C. 2 out of 9

   D. 1 out of 5

2. Which is a way of predicting a probable outcome? (*Circle the correct letter.*)

   A. Saying a quarter will only land on tails when dropped from the air.

   B. A weatherman forecasting a 100% chance for rain.

   C. Saying a whale could fit in a bathtub.

   D. Telling your mom that if she does your homework, you will clean your room.

Name _____ Date _____

1. Michelle is selecting a beach towel to purchase for her vacation. She can choose a red, blue, or green beach towel. She can select the towel in a small, medium, or large size. How many possible combinations of 1 beach towel and 1 size are possible? (*Show your work and circle your final answer.*)

2. Leon has one yellow, one red, one blue, and one purple jawbreaker in a jar. If he grabs 2 jawbreakers without looking, how many possible color combination of jawbreakers are possible? (*Show your work and circle your final answer.*)

Name _____ Date _____

1. Mary, Jennifer, George, and Carry have made up a game involving dominoes. The object of the game is to have the most points at the end of the game. Mary has 18 more points than George. George has twice as many as Carry. Carry has 2 fewer points than Jennifer does. Jennifer has 10 points. Based on this information, who won the game? (*Show your work and circle your final answer.*)

2. Timothy flipped 2 coins in the air and let them land on the ground. How many possible ways could the 2 coins have landed? (*Show your work and circle your final answer.*)

Name _____ **Date** _____

Warm-Up 15

1. Adam is 5 years younger than Sandra. Sandra is 5 years younger than Beth. Beth is 45 years old. How old are Sandra and Adam? (*Show your work and circle your final answers.*)

2. Abby has 1 green, 1 blue, 1 red, 1 yellow, and 1 brown cube. If she selects 1 cube without looking, what is the probability that the cube she selects will **not** be red? (*Circle the correct letter.*)

   A. 0.5   **C.** 0.4

   B. 0.8   **D.** 0.7

Name _____ **Date** _____

Warm-Up 16

1. Out of the 100 customers that entered the ice-cream parlor, 15% ordered the triple sundae. How is 15% written as a fraction? (*Circle your final answer.*)

2. Look at the list of numbers. What is the **range** of the numbers shown? (*Show your work and circle your final answer.*)

   | 8, | 12, | 6, | 6, | 4, | 3, | 8, | 9, | 19, | 9, | 6, | 6, | 18 |

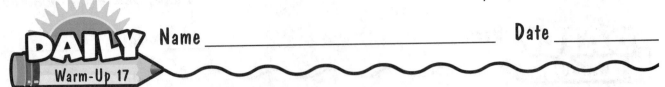

Name _____ **Date** _____

DAILY
Warm-Up 17

1. The forecast for rain today is 95%. The chance of rain is _____ . (*Circle the correct letter.*)

A. certain   **B.** likely   **C.** possible   **D.** not possible

2. Look at the graph. On what 2 consecutive days did the number of tires changed increase the most? (*Circle your final answer.*)

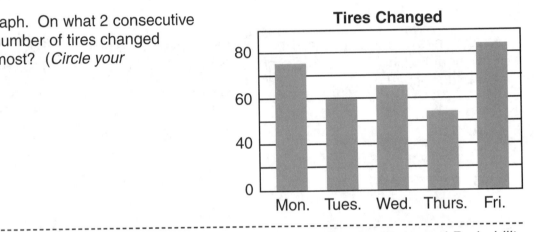

Tires Changed

Name _____ **Date** _____

DAILY
Warm-Up 18

1. Jenna wants to draw a picture. She has 4 crayons, 3 markers, and 3 colored pencils. If she plans to draw her picture with only 1 crayon, 1 marker, and 1 colored pencil, how many possible combinations can she choose from? (*Show your work and circle your final answer.*)

2. Ernest used a spinner that had 2 odd numbers and 2 even numbers. Which spinner below did Ernest use? (*Circle the correct letter.*)

A. 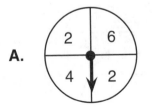   **B.**    **C.**    **D.**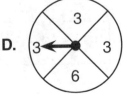

Name _____   **Date** _____

Warm-Up 19

1. Pete has a book of stickers with the letters A, B, or C printed on them. If he grabs 1 sticker without looking, what fraction describes the probability that he will **not** choose a sticker with the letters B or C? (*Circle the correct letter.*)

A $\frac{4}{12}$ **B.** $\frac{2}{6}$ **C.** $\frac{1}{2}$ **D.** $\frac{3}{12}$

2. Misty is practicing shooting her basketball. She made 25 of the 35 shots she attempted. Based on this data, what is the most reasonable prediction of the number of shots Misty will make out of 63 attempts? (*Show your work and circle your final answer.*)

Name _____   **Date** _____

Warm-Up 20

1. The graph shows the number of laps four friends swam in P.E. class. Which statement about the data is **not** correct? (*Circle the correct letter.*)

A. Each friend swam an odd number of laps.

B. Frank swam the least number of laps.

C. Pat swam four more laps than Mark.

D. Mark swam more laps than Frank and Gene combined.

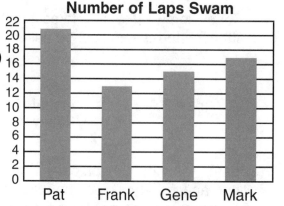

Number of Laps Swam

2. Elias played 8 games of basketball during the week. In the first game, he made 6 baskets. He made 8 baskets in each of the next 4 games. In the next 2 games, he made 5 baskets each game. In the last game Elias played, he made 8 baskets. Find the average number of baskets Elias made. (*Show your work and circle your final answer.*)

Name _____   **Date** _____

Warm-Up 21

1. Of the 36 volleyball members on the high-school team, 8 are graduating this year. If Janet writes all 36 volleyball members' names down on individual pieces of paper and then selects 1 without looking, what is the probability she will select a member of the team who is graduating? (*Show your work and circle your final answer.*)

2. Terry grows roses in her garden. In the first row of her garden, she planted 10 rose bushes. In the second row, she planted twice as many rose bushes as she did in the first row. In the third and fourth rows, she planted the sum of rows 1 and 2. In the fifth row, she planted the sum of rows 1, 2, and 4. How many total rose bushes did Terry plant in her garden? (*Show your work and circle your final answer.*)

- -

Name _____   **Date** _____

Warm-Up 22

1. Today, the weatherman forecasted a 20% chance of thunderstorms. The chance of thunderstorms can best be described as _____ . (*Circle the correct letter.*)

A. impossible   **B.** certain   **C.** likely   **D.** not likely

2. Larry has a bag of apples and oranges. He picked 20 pieces of fruit at random from the bag and put each piece of fruit back as he made a chart of the fruit he picked. Based on these results, what is the best prediction of fruit in the bag? (*Circle the correct letter.*)

A. It is likely that there are more apples than oranges.

B. There are definitely more oranges than apples.

C. There is an equal number of oranges and apples.

D. There are 17 more apples than oranges.

Tally Chart	
Oranges	Apples
II	ʽN̶N̶ ʽN̶N̶ ʽN̶N̶ IIII

DAILY Warm-Up 23

Name _____ Date _____

1. Mrs. Jenkins looked at the grades of five students on four math tests. Find the **mean** of each students' math tests. Write each answer in the table.

Student	Test A	Test B	Test C	Test D	Mean
Nancy	82	73	87	94	
Linda	62	82	73	79	
Jamal	39	63	98	88	
Broderick	98	71	89	74	
Sampson	78	77	67	46	

Who has the highest mean? _____

2. Jerry bought a package of towels for his kitchen. There were 10 green towels, 16 blue towels, and 4 orange towels. If Jerry grabbed 1 towel without looking, what is the probability he will select a blue towel? (*Show your work and circle your final answer.*)

DAILY Warm-Up 24

Name _____ Date _____

1. Janet and Lee played 10 games of basketball. The table shows the number of points each person scored per game. Which statement about the table is **false**? (*Circle the correct letter.*)

	1	2	3	4	5	6	7	8	9	10
Janet	21	14	16	2	28	32	24	22	26	24
Lee	18	24	28	32	12	8	10	14	12	16

A. Janet won more games than Lee.

B. In game 4, Lee scored 30 more points than Janet.

C. Lee won fewer games than Janet.

D. In game 6, Lee scored 24 more points than Janet.

2. Carlos wrote the numbers 1 through 9 on separate cards. He placed each numbered card in a bag. If he grabs 1 numbered card without looking, what is the probability he will select an odd number? (*Circle the correct letter.*)

A. $\frac{2}{9}$ **B.** $\frac{3}{9}$ **C.** $\frac{4}{9}$ **D.** $\frac{5}{9}$

Name _____   **Date** _____

Warm-Up 25

1. Rico is arranging a blue cube, an orange cube, and a yellow cube side by side. Rico made a list of al the possible ways he could arrange the cubes. Which possible arrangement is Rico missing on his list? (*Circle the correct letter.*)

   A. Blue   Orange Yellow

   B. Yellow Blue   Orange

   C. Orange Blue   Yellow

   D. Yellow Orange Blue

Blue	Orange	Yellow
Blue	Yellow	Orange
Yellow	Blue	Orange
Orange	Blue	Yellow
Orange	Yellow	Blue

2. Ron likes to color using crayons. In his crayon box, he has 1 blue crayon, 2 orange crayons, and 2 green crayons. He wants to color a picture for his uncle using 2 of those crayons. List all the ways Ron can color the picture if he doesn't duplicate any color combinations.

Name _____   **Date** _____

Warm-Up 26

1. When Jamal comes home from school each day, he likes to eat a snack. Today, he can choose a tuna or peanut butter sandwich. He can also choose a grape, strawberry, or cola drink. How many possible combinations of 1 sandwich and 1 drink can Jamal choose from? (*Show your work and circle your final answer.*)

2. Sam put a quarter in a gumball machine. In the machine, there are 2 blue, 1 pink, 2 orange, and 2 yellow gumballs. For each quarter inserted into the machine, 2 gumballs come out. How many possible color gumball combinations are possible for Sam to get with his quarter? (*Show your work and circle your final answer.*)

1. Janet, Mark, Paul, and Henry each rode their bikes over the summer. Janet rode 5 less miles than Paul. Mark rode the sum of the miles Janet and Paul rode. Paul rode 13 less miles than Henry. Henry rode 30 miles. How many miles did Janet, Mark, and Paul each ride over the summer? (*Show your work and circle your final answers.*)

2. Brandon and Mitchell are trying to buy a new computer. Altogether, they have $750. Brandon put $160 more towards the computer than Mitchell. How much money have Brandon and Mitchell each put towards the new computer? (*Show your work and circle your final answer.*)

Warm-Up 28

1. Monica won a coupon for a free ice cream. She can choose to have her ice cream in a cone, in a bowl, or on a stick. She can choose chocolate, vanilla, or strawberry ice cream. How many possible combinations can Monica choose to get her free ice cream?

2. Mrs. Henry ordered a box of pencils for her students. The box contained different numbers of pencils that are different colors. The table shows the number and color of pencils Mrs. Henry ordered for the new school year. If Mrs. Henry grabs a pencil without looking, what is the probability she will select a yellow pencil? (*Circle the correct letter.*)

Orange	10
Blue	18
Yellow	20
Red	12

A. $\frac{1}{3}$ **B.** $\frac{3}{10}$ **C.** $\frac{2}{10}$ **D.** $\frac{2}{3}$

Name _____   **Date** _____

Warm-Up 29

1. Rico and Sam practiced tennis for 28 minutes on Monday, 59 minutes on Tuesday, 84 minutes on Wednesday, 49 minutes on Thursday, and 67 minutes on Friday. What is the **median** amount of time that Rico and Sam practiced tennis? (*Show your work and circle your final answer.*)

2. Hector and Leon are playing cards. Leon asked Hector what chance he had for drawing an ace from a standard deck of 52 cards. What chance does Leon have? (*Show your work and circle your final answer.*)

- -

Name _____   **Date** _____

Warm-Up 30

1. Ernest received 7 of his math grades back in Mrs. Long's class. On Test 1, he scored 85%, on Test 2 he scored 80%, on Test 3 he scored 79%, on Test 4 he scored 75%, on Test 5 he scored 82%, on Test 6 he scored 84%, and on Test 7 he scored 80%. Find his **median** score for the math tests. (*Show your work and circle your final answer.*)

2. At the reading awards, 10 white ribbons were awarded, 17 red ribbons were awarded, 16 orange ribbons were awarded, and 13 green ribbons were awarded. What is the **mean** number of ribbons awarded for reading? (*Show your work and circle your final answer.*)

Name _____   **Date** _____

Warm-Up 31

1. As a science project, Roberto is trying to find the best way to show the amount of rainfall in his hometown during the month of May. Which would be the best way to show the data? (*Circle the correct letter.*)

   A. guess and check   **C.** make a graph

   B. make a table   **D.** act it out

2. Jonah had 6 green markers and 4 red markers in his backpack. If Jonah grabs 1 marker without looking, what is the probability that the marker he selects will **not** be red? (*Show your work and circle your final answer.*)

Name _____   **Date** _____

Warm-Up 32

1. Henry gave Mark 20 baseball cards, he gave Sam 30 baseball cards, he gave Jeff 40 baseball cards, and he gave Matthew 50 baseball cards. Each baseball card was dated 1999 and is worth $0.27. Which of the following **cannot** be determined from the information given? (*Circle the correct letter.*)

   A. the number of baseball cards given to Matthew

   B. how much each card is worth

   C. when the cards were dated

   D. the number of baseball cards Henry had in the beginning

2. Matthew has 2 quarters, 2 dimes, and 1 penny in his pocket. If Matthew selects a coin without looking, what is the probability in decimal form that the coin Matthew selects is **not** a dime? (*Show your work and circle your final answer.*)

Name _____   **Date** _____

Warm-Up 33

1. Each year, students in 6th grade participate in "Track Day." Use the clues below to determine which students placed, 1st, 2nd, 3rd, 4th, and 5th in the 440-yard relay?

- Cade finished after Ashton.

- Ashton didn't finish second.

- Libby finished before Marissa but after Cade.

- Marissa finished last.

- Robyn finished right before Marissa.

	Robyn	Ashton	Libby	Marissa	Cade
1st					
2nd					
3rd					
4th					
5th					

2. Terry signed up for a contest. She and 4 friends were chosen as finalists. All finalists are guaranteed to win a prize. Each finalist has the opportunity to win $1,000, a new computer, a home stereo, a $5,000 scholarship, or a new car. If each finalist could only win 1 prize, what is the probability Terry could win a new car? (*Show your work and circle your final answer.*)

Name _____   **Date** _____

Warm-Up 34

1. Duvall has 6 music CDs in his cabinet. He has 2 country CDs, 2 rap CDs, and 2 pop CDs. If Duvall grabs 2 CDs out of the cabinet without looking, how many combinations of CDs are possible? (*Show your work and circle your final answer.*)

2. Terry wrote the letters T, E, N, N, E, S, S, E and E on separate cards. She shuffled the cards, turned them facedown, and flipped 1 card over at a time. The cards below are the ones Terry has already flipped. What is the probability that the next card Terry flips will **not** be an E? (*Circle the correct letter.*)

E	N	T		N	S			

A. 1 out of 4   **B.** 2 out of 4   **C.** 3 out of 4   **D.** 4 out of 4

Name _____ **Date** _____

Warm-Up 35

1. David has 1 red life jacket, 4 blue life jackets, 7 green life jackets, and 9 orange life jackets in a storage area on his boat. If David grabs 1 life jacket from the storage area without looking, what is the probability the life jacket he picks will be green? (*Show your work and circle your final answer.*)

2. Which statement below is correct? (*Circle the correct letter.*)

A. The mode is the difference between the greatest and the least number in a data set.

B. The range is the difference between the least and greatest numbers in a data set.

C. The median is the difference between the greatest and the least number in a data set.

D. The median is the difference between the greatest mode and the least median of a data set.

Name _____ **Date** _____

Warm-Up 36

1. Michael has 6 pens in his backpack. He has 2 green pens, 2 red pens, and 2 blue pens. If Michael grabs 2 pens from his backpack without looking, how many color combinations of pens are possible? (*Show your work and circle your final answer.*)

2. Jennifer calculated one of the answer choices below using the numbers in the box and got 78. Which answer choice did she calculate? (*Circle the correct letter.*)

A. Median

B. Mode

C. Mean

D. Range

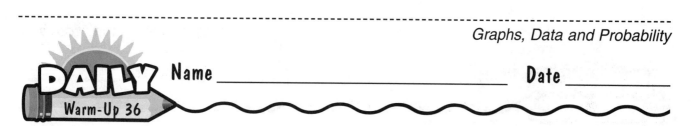

18, 45, 91, 71, 56, 15, 13, 78

DAILY
Warm-Up 37

1. Leon bought a standard deck of 52 cards. If Leon selects 1 card without looking, what is the probability of selecting a black card from the deck? (*Show your work and circle your final answer.*)

2. The number of newspaper subscriptions Nancy sold during a 10-day period is shown on the table. Which of the following functions shows the data of subscriptions sold as 103? (*Circle the correct letter.*)

Day	1	2	3	4	5	6	7	8	9	10
Subscriptions	103	103	104	104	106	102	108	100	101	102

A. Mean   **B.** Mode   **C.** Range   **D.** Median

DAILY
Warm-Up 38

1. Isaac has 3 red, 2 green, 10 blue, 1 orange, and 4 yellow counting chips in a container. If Isaac grabs 1 counting chip without looking, which color chip will he most likely pick? (*Circle the correct letter.*)

A. red   **B.** green   **C.** blue   **D.** orange

2. How can the median of a set of data be found?

_____

_____

_____

Name _____   Date _____

1. Which statement about the mode of a data set is **not** correct? (*Circle the correct letter.*)

   A. The number that appears the most in a data set is the mode.

   B. The number repeated the most in a data set is the mode.

   C. If there are no repeated numbers in a data set, there is no mode.

   D. The mode is the middle number in a data set.

2. How many more pages did Terry, Jack, and Lou read than Sam and Peggy? (*Show your work and circle your final answer.*)

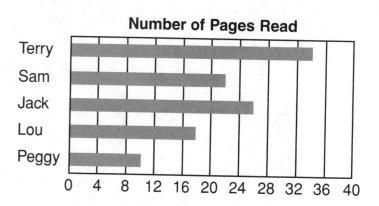

Number of Pages Read

Name _____   Date _____

1. Nick bought a package of jawbreakers containing 4 blue, 3 red, 2 green, and 3 yellow jawbreakers. He gave 1 blue, 1 red, and both green jawbreakers to his brother. If Nick now selects 1 jawbreaker without looking, what is the probability he will **not** select a blue jawbreaker? (*Show your work and circle your final answer.*)

2. Look at the graph. There was a 100% chance of rain predicted for one day this week. Which day did it probably rain? (*Circle your final answer.*)

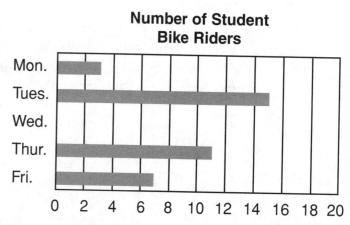

Number of Student Bike Riders

Name _____   **Date** _____

DAILY
Warm-Up 41

1. Janice wrote the numbers 1 through 11 on separate sheets of paper. She then placed each sheet facedown on her desk. If she selects 1 sheet without looking, what is the probability she will select a sheet with an odd number? (*Show your work and circle your final answer.*)

2. During spring break, four friends checked out books from the local library. Jennifer read 100 pages the first night, Greg read 180 pages the first night, Beth read 70 pages less the first night than Greg, and Melanie read 90 more pages the first night than Jennifer. Complete the bar graph showing the number of pages each friend read the first night they checked out their books.

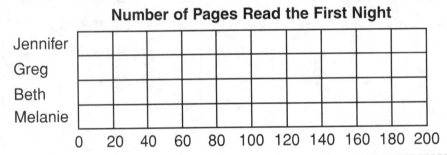

Number of Pages Read the First Night

- -

Name _____   **Date** _____

DAILY
Warm-Up 42

1. Mrs. Thompson wants to compare the month in which students in 6th grade were born. Which answer choice would be best for Mrs. Thompson to organize this data? (*Circle the correct letter.*)

   A. pie chart   **C.** stem and leaf

   B. line graph   **D.** bar graph

2. Amber is a veterinarian. Today, she needs to give medicine to a horse, a dog, and a cat in any order. How many different ways can Amber decide to give the medicine? (*Show your work and circle your final answer.*)

Name _____   **Date** _____

1. After watching a weather forecast, Jack knows there is a 20% chance of rain today. Is the chance for rain likely or unlikely? (*Circle your final answer.*)

2. Chris and Tim are playing a game. Each time they roll a die that lands on an even number, they select a "heads" card. Each time the die lands on an odd number, they select a "tails" card. Chris needs an even number to win the game. What is the probability of Chris rolling an even number? (*Show your work and circle your final answer.*)

┌──────────────┐   ┌──────────────┐
│   **Heads**   │   │   **Tails**   │
│   **Cards**   │   │   **Cards**   │
└──────────────┘   └──────────────┘

Name _____   **Date** _____

1. Yolanda has 10 hair ribbons in her dresser drawer. Three are blue, 4 are green, and 3 are yellow. If Yolanda grabs 1 hair ribbon without looking, what is the probability that she will **not** select a green hair ribbon? (*Show your work and circle your final answer.*)

2. Michael, Lou, and Pete are in a race for 1st, 2nd, and 3rd place. On the table below, show all possible ways of finishing the race.

1st Place	2nd Place	3rd Place

Name _____ **Date** _____

DAILY Warm-Up 45

1. John is buying 2 new shirts. The shirts he likes are hanging on a rack. There are 2 orange, 2 black, and 1 green shirt hanging on the rack. How many color combinations are possible for John to buy his 2 shirts? (*Show your work and circle your final answer.*)

2. Jason is looking for a new sweatshirt for gym class. He can choose between extra-large, large, or medium-sized sweatshirts. He can choose a red, white, or blue sweatshirt. Which diagram shows all the possible combinations of 1 size and 1 color sweatshirt? (*Circle the correct letter.*)

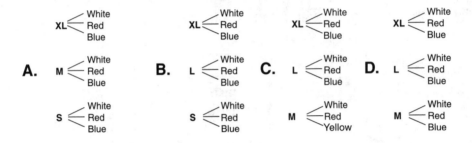

A.
- XL — White, Red, Blue
- M — White, Red, Blue
- S — White, Red, Blue

B.
- XL — White, Red, Blue
- L — White, Red, Blue
- S — White, Red, Blue

C.
- XL — White, Red, Blue
- L — White, Red, Blue
- M — White, Red, Yellow

D.
- XL — White, Red, Blue
- L — White, Red, Blue
- M — White, Red, Blue

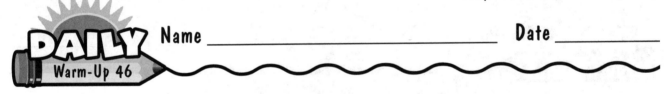

Name _____ **Date** _____

DAILY Warm-Up 46

1. The numbers below show Mark's grades on 8 spelling tests. Mark calculated the _____ of this data and found a result of 84. What did Mark calculate? (*Circle the correct letter.*)

   A. range
   B. median
   C. mode
   D. average

   84, 76, 84, 88, 94, 100, 96, 92

2. Libby wrote the grades she scored on her math homework on a sheet of paper but forgot one grade. She knows the mode of her grades is 92. What is the **median** of Libby's grades? (*Show your work and circle your final answer.*)

Libby's Grades	92, 78, 83, 79, 100, 92, 78, 83, 98, 97, 96, ☐

Name _____ **Date** _____

1. Michael bought a pack of gum with 36 pieces. Nine pieces are strawberry flavored and the rest are grape flavored. If Michael reaches in the pack and selects 1 piece of gum without looking, what is the probability he will select a grape-flavored piece of gum? (*Show your work and circle your final answer.*)

2. Agnes is planting tulips in her flower garden. In the first row, she planted 15 red tulips. In the second row, she planted twice as many blue tulips as the red tulips she planted in the first row. In the third and fourth rows, she planted as many yellow tulips as the sum of the tulips in rows 1 and 2. In the fifth row, she planted as many purple tulips as the sum of the tulips she planted in rows 1, 2, and 4. How many total tulips did Agnes plant in her garden? (*Show your work and circle your final answer.*)

Name _____ **Date** _____

1. Orange County has a 90% chance of heavy rain on Saturday. The chance of rain can best be described as _____ . (*Circle the correct letter.*)

A. impossible   **B.** certain   **C.** likely   **D.** not likely

2. Yolanda bought a package of markers. There are 2 blue markers, 2 green markers, 1 orange marker, 2 red markers, and 2 black markers in the package. If Yolanda selects 2 markers from the package without looking, how many possible color combinations can she get? (*Show your work and circle your final answer.*)

Name _____ **Date** _____

Warm-Up 49

1. Look at the line plot. The line plot shows students' favorite colors in Mr. Wilson's class. Which statement is **not** supported by the information on the line plot? (*Circle the correct letter.*)

   A. More students like the color red, than orange.

   B. More students like the colors red, yellow, and blue than green and orange.

   C. More students like green and red than blue, yellow, and orange.

   D. More students like the colors red and orange than blue, yellow, and green.

	x			
	x	x		
	x	x		
x	x	x		
x	x	x		
x	x	x		
x	x	x		
x	x	x	x	
x	x	x	x	x
x	x	x	x	x
Green	**Red**	**Blue**	**Yellow**	**Orange**

2. Marcie has 3 green hats, 2 yellow hats, and 1 orange hat hanging in her closet. If Marcie grabs 2 hats without looking, how many color combinations are possible if there are no duplicate combinations? (Show your work and circle your final answer.)

Name _____ **Date** _____

Warm-Up 50

1. Rob has 36 quarters in a jar. Inside of the jar, there are 8 quarters dated before 1935. If Rob grabs 1 quarter from the jar without looking, what is the probability that he will select a quarter dated before 1935? (*Show your work and circle your final answer.*)

2. Jennifer has 8 yellow shirts, 4 red shirts, 6 blue shirts, and 6 orange shirts folded in her dresser. Jennifer doesn't like to wear the color red. If Jennifer selects 1 shirt without looking, what is the probability she will **not** select a red shirt? (*Show your work and circle your final answer.*)

DAILY
Warm-Up 51

Name _____ Date _____

1. Ella tossed a quarter 3 times trying to find the probability of the quarter landing on tails on all 3 tosses. What is the probability of the coin landing on tails on all 3 tosses? (*Show your work and circle your final answer.*)

2. The graph shows the number of miles four cousins ran during one week. How many fewer miles did Emily and Jacob run than Robert and Sara? (*Show your work and circle your final answer.*)

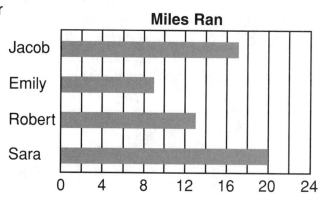

DAILY
Warm-Up 52

Name _____ Date _____

1. Marshal has a bag of colored cubes. There are four green cubes, two gray cubes, and three orange cubes. If Marshal selects 1 colored cube from the bag without looking, what is the probability of selecting a green cube? (*Circle the correct letter.*)

A. 1 out of 9

C. 3 out of 9

B. 2 out of 9

D. 4 out of 9

2. Seth and Jackie are playing a board game. Each time they roll a pair of dice, they advance their game piece according to the number that they roll. Seth needs to roll a 6 and Jackie needs to roll a 4 to each win the game. What is the probability of Seth rolling a 6 and Jackie rolling a 4 with a pair of dice on a single throw? (*Show your work and write your final answers in the boxes.*)

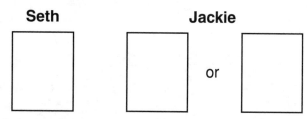

Warm-Up 53

1. Which statement about having a 50% chance of rain is **true**?

A. It is certain to rain.

C. It will definitely rain.

B. It is just as likely to not rain as it is to rain.

D. It will definitely not rain.

2. Heather is graduating from high school. Her mom and dad decided to throw her a graduation party. Heather addressed 45 invitations to friends, 30 invitations to family members, and 25 invitations to friends of her parents. She placed them in a bag for her mother to take to the post office. If Heather selects 1 invitation from the bag without looking, what is the probability of Heather **not** selecting an invitation addressed to her parents' friends? (*Show your work and circle your final answer.*)

- -

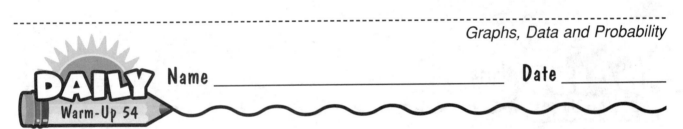

Warm-Up 54

1. David is going camping with his family and friends. He buys 6 orange drinks, 6 grape drinks, 18 lemon-lime drinks, and 6 cranberry drinks and places them in the cooler. If David selects 1 drink from the cooler without looking, what is the probability of him selecting a lemon-lime flavored drink? (*Show your work and circle your final answer.*)

2. Tammy, Scott, Brent, and Katie are running the 100-yard dash in the track meet. How many different ways can they finish 1st, 2nd, 3rd, and 4th? (*Show your work and circle your final answer.*)

DAILY Warm-Up 55

Name _____   Date _____

1. Cindy bought a package of 20 markers. The table below shows the color and number of markers for each color in the package. What is the **median** number of markers in the package? (*Show your work and circle your final answer.*)

Color	Number
Blue	3
Green	6
Yellow	5
Orange	2
Red	4

2. Ana, Kayla, Sarah, Marci, and Petra swam the 50-meter butterfly at the swim meet. Marci finished faster than Sarah but slower than Kayla. Kayla finished before Marci but behind Ana. Petra finished before Kayla but did not finish first. List the order in which they finished the race?

- -

DAILY Warm-Up 56

Name _____   Date _____

1. Coach Erin teaches swimming class at the aquatic center. The table shows the number of students in each of the 6 classes she teaches. What is the **mode** and **mean** of students Coach Erin teaches each period?
(*Circle the correct letter.*)

Class Period	Number of Students
1	24
2	22
3	30
4	28
5	26
6	26

A. Mode: 22   Mean: 24

B. Mode: 26   Mean: 26

C. Mode: 26   Mean: 28

D. Mode: 30   Mean: 39

2. Riley has 3 quarters, 2 dimes, 3 nickels, and 2 pennies in his pocket. If Riley chooses a coin from his pocket without looking, what is the probability he will select a quarter or a dime? (*Show your work and circle your final answer.*)

DAILY
Warm-Up 57

Name _____ Date _____

1. Michael bought a bag of marbles. There were 20 green marbles, 10 yellow marbles, 10 orange marbles, and 10 blue marbles in the bag. If Michael selects 1 marble from the bag without looking, what is the probability he will select an orange marble? (*Show your work and circle your final answer.*)

2. The graph shows the number of water bottles sold over a 4-month period. How many more water bottles were sold during March and February than January and April? (*Show your work and circle your final answer.*)

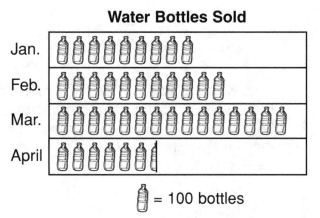

Water Bottles Sold

Jan.
Feb.
Mar.
April

= 100 bottles

DAILY
Warm-Up 58

Name _____ Date _____

1. Kathy's Kite Keepers had a sale on Kites. The graph shows the number of kites sold during 4 days. According to the graph, how many more kites were sold on Monday and Wednesday than on Tuesday and Thursday? (*Show your work and circle your final answer.*)

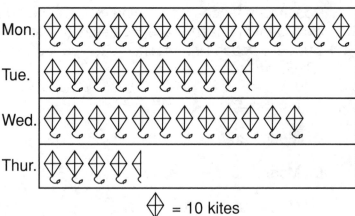

Mon.
Tue.
Wed.
Thur.

= 10 kites

2. Michael earns $9.50 an hour at his job. He worked 8 hours the first week and 14 hours the second week. During weeks three and four, Michael worked 7 more hours (each week) than he did the second week. How much did he earn after 4 weeks of work? (*Show your work and circle your final answer.*)

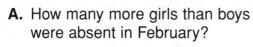

DAILY
Warm-Up 59

Name _____   Date _____

1. Answer the questions by looking at the bar graph.

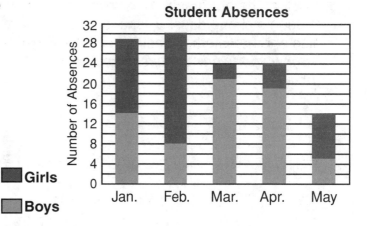

Student Absences

A. How many more girls than boys were absent in February?

_____ girls

B. What is the total number of absent girls during the five months?

_____ girls

■ **Girls**
■ **Boys**

2. Robin, Wanda, Leeann, and Terry all traveled during summer break. Robin traveled 6 miles more than Wanda. Terry traveled 9 miles less than Wanda. Wanda traveled 8 miles more than Leeann. Leeann traveled 84 miles. How many miles did each girl travel? (*Show your work and circle your final answer.*)

DAILY
Warm-Up 60

Name _____   Date _____

1. The grades below show what Pete scored on 9 of his spelling tests. What is the **range** of his grades? (*Show your work and circle your final answer.*)

| 63, 98, 94, 86, 84, 99, 84, 94, 78 |

2. Look at the line graph.

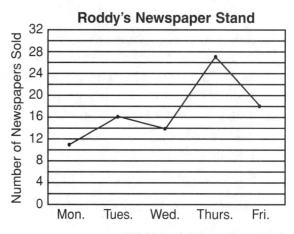

Roddy's Newspaper Stand

A. Which 2 consecutive days showed the greatest increase in sales?

_____

B. On which 2 consecutive days was there the greatest decrease in sales?

_____

Name _____ **Date** _____

Warm-Up 61

1. Look at the bar graph. How many more students chose dogs, cats, and birds than fish and hamsters as their favorite pets? (*Show your work and circle your final answer.*)

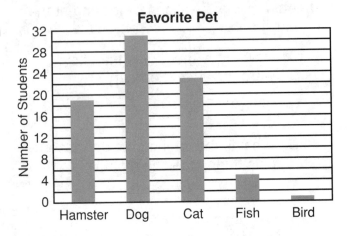

Favorite Pet

2. Ella bought a new book. The table shows the number of minutes she read this week. What is the **mode** for the amount of time Ella read this week? (*Circle your final answer.*)

	Monday	Tuesday	Wednesday	Thursday	Friday	Saturday	Sunday
Minutes Read	20	28	17	28	14	20	28

- -

Name _____ **Date** _____

Warm-Up 62

1. Grace delivers newspapers every Sunday. The table shows the number of newspapers she delivered during four months. What is the **average** number of newspapers Grace delivered during the four months? (*Show your work and circle your final answer.*)

	September	October	November	December
Papers Delivered	94	122	102	142

2. The bar graph shows the color and number of balloons at Josh's birthday party. What is the difference between the number of yellow balloons and orange balloons at the party? (*Show your work and circle your final answer.*)

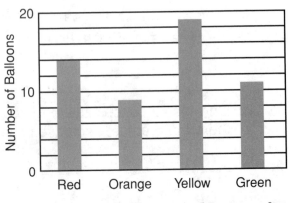

Graphs, Data and Probability

Answer Key

Warm-Up 1
1. B
2. $\frac{5}{8}$

Warm-Up 2
1. 6 combinations
2.

Warm-Up 3
1. 6 color combinations
2. 6 ways

Warm-Up 4
1. $\frac{1}{6}$
2. 84

Warm-Up 5
1. B
2. D

Warm-Up 6
1. 6 combinations
2. vanilla, chocolate
vanilla, strawberry
vanilla, vanilla
chocolate, strawberry
chocolate, chocolate

Warm-Up 7
1. A
2. $\frac{1}{12}$

Warm-Up 8
1. 8 combinations
2. The chance for rain is likely.

Warm-Up 9
1. $\frac{1}{13}$
2. $\frac{1}{4}$ or 25%

Warm-Up 10
1. C
2. D

Warm-Up 11
1. C
2. $\frac{2}{9}$

Warm-Up 12
1. A
2. B

Warm-Up 13
1. 9 combinations
2. 6 color combinations

Warm-Up 14
1. Mary
2. 4 ways

Warm-Up 15
1. Sandra: 40 years
Adam: 35 years
2. B

Warm-Up 16
1. $\frac{15}{100} = \frac{3}{20}$
2. 16

Warm-Up 17
1. B
2. Thursday and Friday

Warm-Up 18
1. 36 combinations
2. B

Warm-Up 19
1. C
2. 45 shots

Warm-Up 20
1. D
2. 7 baskets

Warm-Up 21
1. $\frac{2}{9}$
2. 150 rose bushes

Warm-Up 22
1. D
2. A

Warm-Up 23
1. Nancy = 84
Linda = 74

Jamal = 72
Broderick = 83
Sampson = 67
Highest mean = Nancy
2. $\frac{8}{15}$

Warm-Up 24
1. D
2. D

Warm-Up 25
1. D
2. blue, orange
blue, green
orange, orange
orange, green
green, green

Warm-Up 26
1. 6 combinations
2. 9 color combinations

Warm-Up 27
1. Janet: 12 miles
Mark: 29 miles
Paul: 17 miles
2. Answers may vary.
Possible answer:
Brandon: $455
Mitchell: $295

Warm-Up 28
1. 9 combinations
2. A

Warm-Up 29
1. 59 minutes
2. $\frac{1}{13}$

Warm-Up 30
1. 80%
2. 14 ribbons

Warm-Up 31
1. C
2. $\frac{3}{5}$

Warm-Up 32
1. D
2. 0.6

Graphs, Data
and Probability

Answer Key

Warm-Up 33

1.

	Robyn	Ashton	Libby	Marissa	Cade
1st		✔			
2nd					✔
3rd			✔		
4th	✔				
5th				✔	

2. $\frac{1}{5}$

Warm-Up 34
1. 6 combinations
2. A

Warm-Up 35
1. $\frac{1}{3}$
2. B

Warm-Up 36
1. 6 color combinations
2. D

Warm-Up 37
1. $\frac{1}{2}$
2. D

Warm-Up 38
1. C
2. The middle value in a list of numbers ordered from least to greatest or greatest to least.

Warm-Up 39
1. D
2. 46 more pages

Warm-Up 40
1. $\frac{5}{8}$
2. Wednesday

Warm-Up 41
1. $\frac{6}{11}$
2.

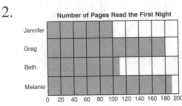

Number of Pages Read the First Night

Warm-Up 42
1. D
2. 6 ways

Warm-Up 43
1. unlikely
2. 50% or $\frac{1}{2}$

Warm-Up 44
1. $\frac{3}{5}$
2.

1st Place	2nd Place	3rd Place
Michael	Lou	Pete
Michael	Pete	Lou
Lou	Michael	Pete
Lou	Pete	Michael
Pete	Michael	Lou
Pete	Lou	Michael

Warm-Up 45
1. 5 color combinations
2. D

Warm-Up 46
1. C
2. 92

Warm-Up 47
1. $\frac{3}{4}$
2. 225 tulips

Warm-Up 48
1. C
2. 14 color combinations

Warm-Up 49
1. D
2. 5 color combinations

Warm-Up 50
1. $\frac{2}{9}$
2. $\frac{5}{6}$

Warm-Up 51
1. $\frac{1}{8}$ 2. 7 fewer miles

Warm-Up 52
1. D
2. Seth: $\frac{5}{36}$

Jackie: $\frac{3}{36}$ or $\frac{1}{12}$

Warm-Up 53
1. B
2. $\frac{3}{4}$

Warm-Up 54
1. $\frac{1}{2}$
2. 24 ways

Warm-Up 55
1. 4
2. Ana, Petra, Kayla, Marci, and Sarah

Warm-Up 56
1. B
2. $\frac{1}{2}$

Warm-Up 57
1. $\frac{1}{5}$
2. 1,050 more water bottles

Warm-Up 58
1. 120 more kites
2. $608

Warm-Up 59
1. A. 14 girls
   B. 54 girls
2. Robin: 89 miles
   Wanda: 92 miles
   Terry: 83 miles
   Leeann: 84 miles

Warm-Up 60
1. 36
2. A. Wednesday and Thursday
   B. Thursday and Friday

Warm-Up 61
1. 31 more students
2. 28 minutes

Warm-Up 62
1. 115 newspapers
2. 10 balloons

ALGEBRA, PATTERNS AND FUNCTIONS

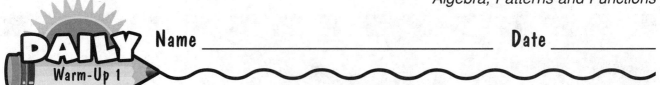

Name _____ **Date** _____

1. Samantha and Beth own a hair salon. Beth gave 252 haircuts during a 6-month period. The ratio of haircuts Samantha gave to the haircuts Beth gave is 3 to 1. How many haircuts during the 6-month period did Samantha give? (*Show your work and circle your final answer.*)

2. Jenny makes bracelets out of beads for her friends. The table shows how many beads she will need for different numbers of bracelets. Which equation can be used to find *b*, the number of beads needed to make *n* number of bracelets? (*Circle the correct letter.*)

A. $72n = b$

B. $24n = b$

C. $b = 24 - n$

D. $b = n + 24$

Number of Bracelets	Number of Beads
3	72
5	120
7	168
9	216
11	264

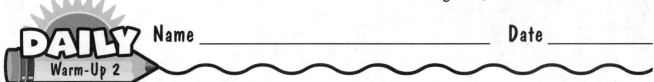

Name _____ **Date** _____

1. Sandy is collecting seashells at the beach. She found 24 small seashells and 18 large seashells. What ratio compares the number of small seashells to the number of large seashells she found on the beach? (*Show your work and circle your final answer.*)

2. Katie's dog, Lola, had puppies. Lola had 6 male puppies and 4 female puppies. The ratio of the number of female puppies to the number of male puppies is $\frac{4}{6}$. Simplify this fraction. (*Show your work and circle your final answer.*)

Name _____   **Date** _____

1. Solve each problem below. (*Show your work and circle your final answers.*)

A. $\sqrt{100} \div \sqrt{25}$ **B.** $\sqrt{16} \times \sqrt{64}$

2. Ms. Kovar wrote the numbers in the box below on the board of her classroom. She asked her students to find which number sentence could be used to find *y*, the eighth number in the pattern. (*Circle the correct letter.*)

A. $18 + 8 = y$ **C.** $18 \times 8 = y$

B. $18 - 8 = y$ **D.** $18 \div 8 = y$

$$18, \quad 36, \quad 54, \quad 72, \quad 90, \ldots$$

Name _____   **Date** _____

1. Marsha has 696 pennies in a jar. Marsha selects 24 pennies at random and finds that 13 are dated before 1945. Based on her findings, what is the best prediction of the total number of pennies in the jar that are dated before 1945? (*Show your work and circle your final answer.*)

2. Jim is collecting aluminum cans. So far, he has collected 666 cans. When bagging the cans to take to the recycling center, he noticed that out of the first 18 cans he examined, 10 were red. Based on Jim's observation, what is the best prediction of the total number of cans that are red? (*Show your work and circle your final answer.*)

DAILY Warm-Up 5   **Name** _____   **Date** _____

1. Solve the problems below.

    A. 27 cm + y = 132 cm y = _____ cm   **C.** 47 cm + w = 162 cm w = _____ cm

    B. z + 56 mm = 189 mm z = _____ mm   **D.** x – 76 mm = 231 mm x = _____ mm

2. Lee is building a bookshelf for his living room. He needs 2 boards with a total length of $5\frac{3}{4}$ feet. The first board is $1\frac{3}{8}$ feet long. How long does the second board need to be? (*Show your work and circle your final answer.*)

DAILY Warm-Up 6   **Name** _____   **Date** _____

1. In which problem does y represent the number 100? (*Circle the correct letter.*)

    A. Problem A

    B. Problem B   **A.** $1.3y = 130$ **B.** $\dfrac{130}{y} = 1.3$

    C. Both problems

    D. Neither problem

2. Find the missing values in the problems below. (*Show your work and circle your final answers.*)

    A. $4\frac{3}{8} - y = 3\frac{1}{4}$ **B.** $1 = \frac{4}{3}z$

Name _____ **Date** _____

Warm-Up 7

1. Look at the table. Which expression best describes the value of *m* in terms of the value of *n*? (*Circle the correct letter.*)

n	2	3	4	5	6	7	8
m	11	15	19	23	27	31	35

A. $n + 9 = m$ **B.** $4n + 4 = m$ **C.** $4n - 3 = m$ **D.** $4n + 3 = m$

2. Look at the pattern of numbers. Heather is trying to find the seventh number in the pattern. Which number sentence can Heather use to find *z*, the seventh number in the pattern? (*Circle the correct letter.*)

A. $z = 15 \times 7$

B. $z = 15 + 7$

C. $z - 15 - 7$

D. none of the above

$$15, \quad 30, \quad 50, \quad 70, \ldots$$

Name _____ **Date** _____

Warm-Up 8

1. Chelsea bought a box of beads for making necklaces. The box has 920 beads. After taking out 40 beads at random, she notices that 19 of the beads are blue. Based on Chelsea's observation, what is the best prediction of the total number of blue beads that are in the box that Chelsea bought? (S*how your work and circle your final answer.*)

2. Abigail wants to go skating with her friends. Her mom told her she needed to stay home to study her math. Abigail told her that she felt confident she would score 100% on her next test. Abigail's mom told her if she could correctly work the problem below, she could go skating. Did Abigail get to go skating?
(*Circle your final answer.*)

$$(15 \times 30) \div (30 - 15)$$

Abigail's Work
$(15 \times 30) \div (30 - 15)$
$450 \div 15$
$\begin{array}{r} 15 \\ \times\ 30 \\ \hline 450 \end{array}$ $\qquad$ $\begin{array}{r} 30 \\ 15\overline{)450} \\ -45 \\ \hline 00 \\ -0 \\ \hline 0 \end{array}$
Answer = 30

1. In gym class, there is 1 kickball for every 12 students. Altogether, there are 672 students. Which proportion below will correctly find *n*, the number of kickballs there are in gym class? (*Circle the correct letter.*)

A. $\dfrac{n}{672} = \dfrac{1}{12}$ **B.** $\dfrac{n}{12} = \dfrac{1}{672}$ **C.** $\dfrac{n}{1} = \dfrac{12}{672}$ **D.** $\dfrac{12}{n} = \dfrac{1}{672}$

2. Henry has a collection of music CDs. Upon categorizing his CDs, he finds 0.45 of his CDs are country music. Which statement is correct about the fraction of CDs that are country music? (*Circle the correct letter.*)

A. 9 out of every 20 CDs are country music.

B. 4 out of every 20 CDs are country music.

C. 25 CDs are country music.

D. none of the above

1. Of the students in Mr. Riley's math class, 0.7 of the students scored 100% on their tests. What percent of the students scored 100% on their tests? (*Show your work and circle your final answer.*)

2. Solve the problems below. (*Show your work and write your final answers on the lines.*)

A. June is watching deer grazing in a field. Of the 20 deer in the field, 12 stop grazing when she stops her car in front of the field. What percent of the deer stopped grazing when June stopped her car in front of the field?

_____ %

B. Cameron invited 25 friends to his 16th birthday party. Of the friends invited, 19 came to the party. What percent of the friends Cameron invited came to his party?

_____ %

Name _____ **Date** _____

Warm-Up 11

1. Tyler's cousin Brandi is 5 years older than twice Tyler's age. If *y* represents Tyler's age and *n* represents Brandy's age, which equation shows the relationship between Tyler and Brandy's age? (*Circle the correct letter.*)

   A. $y = 2n - 5$ **C.** $y = 2n + 5$

   B. $n = 2y + 5$ **D.** $n = 2y - 5$

2. Frank owns a lawnmower shop. By the end of April, the ratio of riding mowers to push mowers sold was 3:1. If Frank sold a total of 156 riding mowers during the month of April, how many push mowers did he sell? (*Show your work and circle your final answer.*)

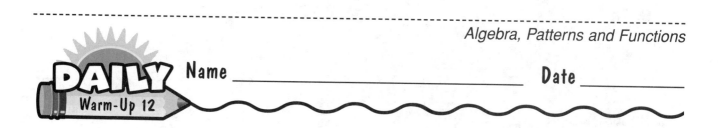

Name _____ **Date** _____

Warm-Up 12

1. Janet owns a flower shop. During the month of February, the ratio of roses to carnations sold was 4:1. If there were a total of 943 carnations sold, how many roses did Janet sell? (*Show your work and circle your final answer.*)

2. Look at the table. Which equation can be used to find the relationship between column *y* and column *x*? (*Circle the correct letter.*)

   A. $y = 3x$ **C.** $x = 6y$

   B. $x = y + 6$ **D.** $y = 6x$

y	x
3	18
5	30
7	42
9	54
11	66
13	78

Name _____ **Date** _____

DAILY Warm-Up 13

1. Solve the problems below. (*Show your work and circle your final answers.*)

A. $1 - n = \dfrac{7}{12}$

B. $\dfrac{3^2 + 4^2}{5}$

2. Which equation states that 2 less than 7 times some number is equal to 70? (*Circle the correct letter.*)

A. $2 - 7n = 70$

C. $70 - 7n = 2$

B. $7n - 2 = 70$

D. $2 + 7n = 70$

Name _____ **Date** _____

DAILY Warm-Up 14

1. Look at the pattern in the table. What is the value of *x* when *w* is 13? (*Show your work and circle your final answer.*)

w	x
7	42
10	60
13	?
16	96

2. Look at the equation below. What value of *z* makes the equation true? (*Circle the correct letter.*)

A. 10   **C.** 8

B. 9   **D.** 7

$$7z + 1 = 50$$

Name _____ **Date** _____

Warm-Up 15

1. At a shoe store, 25 customers came in during the first hour, 14 customers during the second hour, 20 customers during the third hour, 18 customers during the fourth hour, and 33 customers during the fifth hour. What is the **mean** number of customers that came in the store each hour? (*Show your work and circle your final answer.*)

2. Two of Mandy's hamsters had a total of 20 baby hamsters altogether. Mandy gave 4 of her friends 3 hamsters each. A week later, another of Mandy's hamsters had 6 more babies. Which equation can be used to find the number of baby hamsters Mandy has now? (*Circle the correct letter.*)

A. 20 − (4 x 3) + 6

C. 20 x (4 x 3) − 6

B. 20 + (4 x 3) + 6

D. 20 x (4 x 3) + 6

Name _____ **Date** _____

Warm-Up 16

1. Look at the table. Which expression can be used to find the *x* value, in relation to the *y* value? (*Circle the correct letter.*)

x	y
1	5
4	14
8	26
13	41
19	59

A. $5x + 2 = y$

C. $3x + 2 = y$

B. $4y + 2 = x$

D. $2y + 2 = x$

2. Jeffrey rides his bike every day. He can ride 5 miles in 40 minutes. If he continues riding his bike at the same rate, how many miles can Jeffrey ride in 2 hours? (*Show your work and circle your final answer.*)

Name _____ **Date** _____

Warm-Up 17

1. Jim is on a basketball team. The box below shows the number of points he scored during numerous games. What is the average number of points Jim scored? (*Show your work and circle your final answer.*)

12, 14, 10, 8, 6, 22

2. Leon wrote the pattern of numbers below. What is the missing number in Leon's pattern?

28, 22, 16, 10, _____

Name _____ **Date** _____

Warm-Up 18

1. George had $10 when he left for school. At lunchtime, he bought a hamburger combo and a chocolate shake. On his way home from school, he bought a soda and a hot dog. When he arrived home, he only had $0.87 left. How much money did George spend that day? (*Show your work and circle your final answer.*)

2. Jared wrote the clues to his mystery number on the paper below. What is Jared's mystery number? (*Show your work and circle your final answer.*)

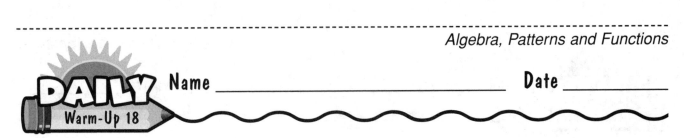

> **When the sixth multiple of 6 is subtracted from the ninth multiple of 4, what is the number?**

Name _____ **Date** _____

1. Solve the problem below. (*Show your work and circle your final answer.*)

$$9^2 - \sqrt{36} + (14 + 14) \div 2^2$$

2. Look at the number pattern. What are the next three numbers in the pattern?

8, 16, 24, 32, _____ , _____ , _____

- -

Name _____ **Date** _____

1. Solve the problem below. (*Circle the correct letter.*)

   A. $n = 4$

   B. $n = 5$

   C. $n = 6$ $3n \times 2 = 42$

   D. $n = 7$

2. If $x = 6$, what is the value of $5x + 7$? (*Show your work and circle your final answer.*)

Warm-Up 21

1. Ernest subtracted a mystery number from 5 and got ⁻4. What mystery number did Ernest use? (*Show your work and circle your final answer.*)

2. Solve the problem below. (*Circle the correct letter.*)

A. $n = 9$ **C.** $n = {}^-9$

$${}^-2n \times 4 = 72$$

B. $n = 8$ **D.** $n = {}^-8$

Warm-Up 22

1. Katie bought a new aquarium in which she placed 15 new fish. Three of the fish were yellow and the rest were black. What is the ratio of yellow fish to the number of black fish in the aquarium? (*Circle the correct letter.*)

A. 4 to 5   **C.** 2 to 5

B. 3 to 5   **D.** 1 to 4

2. Students in 6th grade are selling boxes of apples as a fundraiser. The numbers below show the number of boxes each of the twenty students in Mr. Wilson's class sold. What is the range, mode, and median of boxes sold? (*Show your work and circle your final answers.*)

26, 12, 8, 8, 13, 40, 36, 17, 10, 12, 12, 15, 37, 12, 32, 26, 24, 28, 12, 26

Name _____ **Date** _____

1. Brenda charges $8 for each child she baby-sits, plus an additional $6 an hour. Brenda uses the formula $B = 8 + 6h$ to calculate B, the amount of money she charges for babysitting. If h represents the number of hours she baby-sits, how much money will Brenda make if she baby-sits for 7 hours? (*Show your work and circle your final answer.*)

2. In the gym at Jackson Elementary, there is 1 basketball for every 10 students. If there are 540 students, what proportion can be used to find b, the number of basketballs in the gym? (*Circle the correct letter.*)

A. $\frac{10}{1} = \frac{b}{540}$ **C.** $\frac{1}{10} = \frac{b}{540}$

B. $\frac{540}{1} = \frac{b}{10}$ **D.** $\frac{b}{1} = \frac{10}{540}$

Name _____ **Date** _____

1. Bob read a sign for bike rentals and found that there is a $30 deposit plus an additional $6 an hour for each hour the bike is used. Which expression can be used to find m, the cost of the bike rental for h hours? (*Circle the correct letter.*)

A. $m = 6h + \$30$ **C.** $m = (6 - h) + \$30$

B. $m = 6 + \$30h$ **D.** $m = (6 + h) - \$30$

2. What is the **mean** of the data set below? (*Show your work and circle your final answer.*)

$$8, \quad 2, \quad 1, \quad 9, \quad 4, \quad 6$$

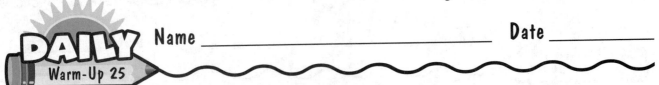

Name _____   **Date** _____

1. Jennifer has 6 green hair ribbons and 15 yellow hair ribbons. Find the ratio of green hair ribbons to yellow hair ribbons as a fraction reduced to lowest terms. (*Show your work and circle your final answer.*)

2. Daniel emptied his piggy bank. He counted 50 quarters, 100 nickels, and 30 pennies. What is the ratio of the number of quarters to total coins in the piggy bank? (*Show your work and circle your final answer.*)

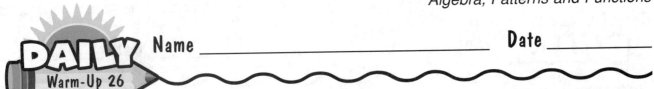

Name _____   **Date** _____

1. Travis wrote the two ratios below on a sheet of paper. Do these two ratios form a proportion? (*Circle your final answer.*)

$$\frac{3}{12} \qquad \frac{6}{24}$$

2. In Michael's baseball card collection, he has 1 baseball card worth $250 for every 3 baseball cards worth $100. If Michael has 6 baseball cards worth $250 in his collection, how many baseball cards does Michael have worth $100? (*Show your work and circle your final answer.*)

Name _____ **Date** _____

DAILY Warm-Up 27

1. Presley's sister Alicia is 4 years older than twice Presley's age. If *x* represents Presley's age and *z* represents Alicia's age, which equation shows the relationship between Presley's and Alicia's ages? (*Circle the correct letter.*)

   A. $x = 2z - 4$ **C.** $x = 2z + 4$

   B. $z = 2x + 4$ **D.** $z = 2x - 4$

2. Mitch is a car salesman. By the end of the year, the ratio of cars to trucks sold was 3:1. If Mitch sold a total of 156 trucks last year, how many cars did he sell? (*Show your work and circle your final answer.*)

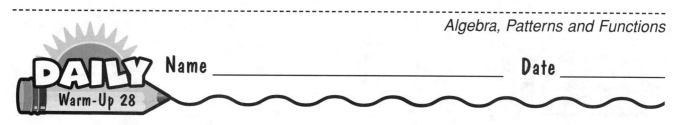

Name _____ **Date** _____

DAILY Warm-Up 28

1. Michael works for a snow-cone shop during the summer. During the month of May, the ratio of cherry to grape snow cones was 4:1. If Michael made a total of 943 grape snow cones, how many cherry snow cones did he make? (*Show your work and circle your final answer.*)

2. Jackie works at an animal adoption center. Four out of every 12 dogs that are brought to the adoption center are puppies. If there are 162 dogs at the adoption center, how many are puppies? (*Show your work and circle your final answer.*)

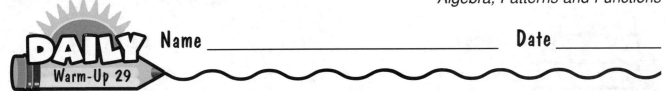

Name _____ **Date** _____

Warm-Up 29

1. At an egg hunt, 2 out of every 3 eggs Jill found were dyed purple. If Jill found a total of 36 eggs, how many eggs can be predicted as being purple? (*Show your work and circle your final answer.*)

2. Cassidy took a math test on Thursday and scored 25%. Friday, she retook the test and got a score of 75%. If there were 100 questions on the test, how many more questions did Cassidy get right on the Friday test than on the Thursday test? (*Show your work and circle your final answer.*)

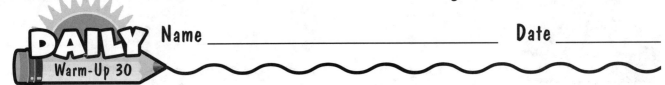

Name _____ **Date** _____

Warm-Up 30

1. Linda is a hair stylist. Of the 20 customers she saw on Saturday, she only shampooed 8. What percent of the customers did Linda shampoo? (*Show your work and circle your final answer.*)

2. Look at the table. What expression represents the *x*-value in terms of the *w*-value? (*Circle the correct letter.*)

A. $6w - 4 = x$ **C.** $6w + 3 = x$

B. $3w + 6 = x$ **D.** $6w - 3 = x$

w	x
2	9
4	21
6	33
8	45

DAILY
Warm-Up 31

Name _____ Date _____

1. Look at the table. What expression represents the *y*-value in terms of the *w*-value?
(*Circle the correct letter.*)

w	y
2	12
4	24
6	36
7	42

A. $4w = y$ **C.** $8w = y$

B. $6w = y$ **D.** $10w = y$

2. While practicing her basketball skills, Courtney is trying to find out how many baskets she can make in 8 minutes. During the first minute, Courtney made 12 baskets. During the second minute, Courtney made 14 baskets. During the third minute, Courtney made 16 baskets, and during the fourth minute, Courtney made 18 baskets. If the number of baskets made continues, how many baskets will Courtney make during the eighth minute? (*Show your work and circle your final answer.*)

DAILY
Warm-Up 32

Name _____ Date _____

1. Look at the function machine. If the "IN" number is 25, what will the "OUT" number be? (*Show your work and circle your final answer.*)

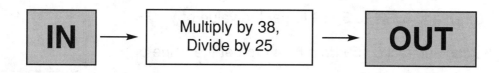

IN → Multiply by 38, Divide by 25 → OUT

2. Sue bought a gallon of milk at the store. After paying with $10, she received $6.94 in change. Which equation below can be used to find *M*, the cost of the gallon of milk?

A. $M = \$10 + \$6.94$ **C.** $M = \$6.94 - \$3.06$

B. $M = \$6.94 + \$3.06$ **D.** $M = \$10 - \$6.94$

Name _____

Date _____

1. Margaret wrote the number pattern below. She asked Robin what number sentence could be used to find *n*, the tenth number in the pattern. (*Circle the correct letter.*)

A. 7 x 63 = *n*

B. 7 x 10 = *n*

C. 63 x 10 = *n*

D. 63 – 9 = *n*

7, 14, 21, 28, 35, ___ , ___ , ___ , ___ , ___ ?

2. Write four number sentences for the numbers 132, 12, and 11.

_____ ÷ _____ = _____   _____ X _____ = _____

_____ ÷ _____ = _____   _____ X _____ = _____

- -

Name _____

Date _____

1. Petra wrote the problem below on the board. How can Petra find the value of *y*?

A. She can subtract 6,144 from 5,159 to get the value of *y*.

B. She can add 6,144 to 5,159 to get the value of *y*.

C. She can subtract 5,159 from 6,144 to get the value of *y*.

D. She can add 6,144 to the value of *y*.

$6{,}144 - y = 5{,}159$

2. Find the missing numbers in the pattern.

	6,144	1,536	384		24	6

Name _____

Date _____

1. Jackson has a photo album of his trip to the White House in Washington, D.C. The album holds 180 photos. There are 20 pages in the album. Which number sentence should be used to find *Z*, the number of photos on each page? (*Circle the correct letter.*)

A. $180 + 20 = Z$

C. $180 - 20 = Z$

B. $180 \div 20 = Z$

D. $180 \times 20 = Z$

2. Jeremiah is playing a video game. For each level he advances, he earns the same number of points. Jeremiah has already advanced to level 15 of the game. He now has a total of 5,350 points. Which number sentence can be used to find *P*, the number of points earned at each level of the game? (*Circle the correct letter.*)

A. $5,350 \times 15 = P$

C. $5,350 + 15 = P$

B. $5,350 - 15 = P$

D. $5,350 \div 15 = P$

Name _____

Date _____

1. Wanda is sewing a blanket out of the fabric her grandmother gave her. She knows the length of her bed is 7 ft. and the width is 6 ft. She wants the length of the blanket to have a 2-foot overlap on each side, and the width to have a 4-foot overlap on each side compared to the length and width of her bed. Which equation can be used to find *A*, the **area** of the blanket Wanda is sewing? (*Circle the correct letter.*)

A. $7 \times 6 = A$

C. $9 \times 10 = A$

B. $11 \times 14 = A$

D. $9 \times 6 = A$

2. Of the 60 rose bushes Margo planted last summer, only 25 survived the snow season. What is the ratio of the number of rose bushes that survived the freeze to the number of rose bushes Margo planted? (*Circle the correct letter.*)

A. 5 out of 12

C. 5 out of 5

B. 5 out of 6

D. 1 out of 5

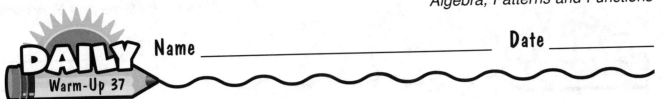

Warm-Up 37

1. What would be the next two shapes in the pattern? (*Circle the correct letter.*)

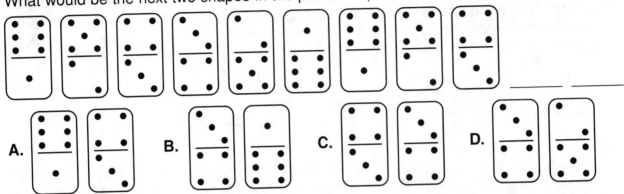

A.   **B.**   **C.**   **D.**

2. The ratio of trucks to cars parked at a parking lot is 7 to 6. There were 28 trucks parked in the parking lot, how many cars were also parked there? (*Show your work and circle your final answer.*)

Warm-Up 38

1. At a pet store, 2 out of every 3 dogs sold were registered Labrador puppies. If there were a total of 36 puppies sold at the pet store, how many puppies can be predicted to be registered Labrador puppies? (*Show your work and circle your final answer.*)

2. Look at the table. What expression represents the *x*-values in terms of the *w*-values? (*Circle the correct letter.*)

A. $4w - 4 = x$ **C.** $4w + 3 = x$

B. $4w \div 4 = x$ **D.** $4w - 3 = x$

w	x
4	12
6	20
8	28
10	36

Warm-Up 39

1. Mrs. Mann went shopping for material her students needed for a science experiment on electricity. Since she needs 12 batteries for 1 group of students, Mrs. Mann decided to buy 72 batteries to be used by the 6 groups she is planning to have do the experiment. What proportion describes this situation? (*Show your work and circle your final answer.*)

2. Kurt collects baseball caps. He has 7 red baseball caps for every 12 blue baseball caps in his collection. If Kurt has 60 blue baseball caps in his collection, how many red baseball caps does Kurt have? (*Show your work and circle your final answer.*)

Warm-Up 40

1. The table shows the number of pages six friends read from a book their teacher assigned. What is the **mean** number of pages read?
(*Show your work and circle your final answer.*)

Friend	Pages
Pete	16
Jack	25
Joy	22
Marissa	27
Courtney	28
Jim	32

2. Look at the number pattern. What are the next three numbers in the pattern?

12,   18,   24,   30,   36, _____ , _____ , _____

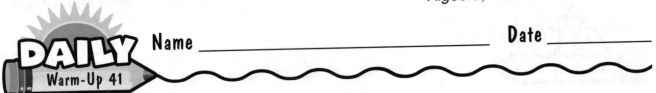

1. Jason is going fishing. The ratio of the number of yellow fishing lures to the number of silver fishing lures he is taking is 6:14. Simplify this ratio. (*Show your work and circle your final answer.*)

2. Fifty people tried out for a new play. Fifteen of them were men and the rest were women. What ratio compares the number of women to the total number of men trying out for the play? (*Show your work and circle your final answer.*)

---

1. In the P.E. department, there are 2 footballs for every 8 basketballs. If Coach Dave counted 12 footballs, how many basketballs did he count? (*Show your work and circle your final answer.*)

2. Look at the table. Which equation can be used to find the relationship between column y and column x? (*Circle the correct letter.*)

A. $x = 5y + 3$ **C.** $x = 5y - 3$

B. $x = y + 5 - 3$ **D.** $y = 5x + 3$

y	x
6	27
7	32
8	37
9	42
10	47
11	52

 **Name** _____ **Date** _____

Warm-Up 43

1. Look at the table. Which expression can be used to represent the value of *m* as related to the value of *n*? (*Circle the correct letter.*)

m	n
3	15
4	19
5	23
6	27
7	31
8	35
9	39

A. $4m + 3 = n$ **C.** $3n + 3 = m$

B. $5m = n$ **D.** $4n + 3 = m$

2. Henry ordered 6 large boxes of oil for the gas station he owns. There were 8 smaller boxes in each large box with 45 bottles of oil in each smaller box. Which equation can be used to find *B*, the number of bottles of oil Henry ordered altogether? (*Circle the correct letter.*)

A. $B = 6 \times 30 \times 45$ **C.** $B = 6 \times 8 \times 45$

B. $B = 8 + 6 + 45$ **D.** $B = 8 - 6 + 45$

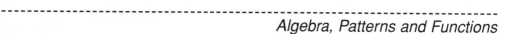

 **Name** _____ **Date** _____

Warm-Up 44

1. Of the 60 cars parked in the school parking lot, only 25 of the cars are yellow. What is the ratio of the number of yellow cars to the total number of cars parked in the parking lot? (*Circle the correct letter.*)

A. 5 out of 12   **C.** 5 out of 11

B. 5 out of 6   **D.** 1 out of 5

2. Linda needs a box of cereal for her children's breakfast. She goes to the store and selects the brand her children like. After paying with $20, she receives $16.94 in change. Which equation below can be used to find *C*, the cost of the cereal Linda purchased? (*Circle the correct letter.*)

A. $C = \$20 + \$16.94$ **C.** $C = \$16.94 + \$3.06$

B. $C = \$16.94 \times \$3.06$ **D.** $C = \$20 - \$16.94$

Name _____   **Date** _____

Warm-Up 45

1. George bought a box of 50 pieces of chocolate. He gave 3 of his sisters 2 pieces of chocolate each. He then gave 2 of his friends 4 pieces of chocolate each. Which equation can be used to find n, the number of pieces of chocolate George has left? (*Circle the correct letter.*)

A. $50 - (3 \times 2) - (2 \times 4) = n$ **C.** $50 - (2 \times 4) = n$

B. $50 - (3 \times 2) = n$ **D.** $50 - (3 \times 2) + (2 \times 4) = n$

2. Which expression represents the x-values in terms of the w-values on the table below? (*Circle the correct letter.*)

A. $x = w + 2$

B. $x = w - 2$

C. $x = w + 4$

D. $x = w - 4$

w	3	12	21	30	39	48
x	1	10	19	28	37	46

Name _____   **Date** _____

Warm-Up 46

1. Mandy and Sam played a game with a dollar's worth of pennies. Mandy won 0.4 of the pennies. Sam won the rest of the pennies. What percent of the pennies did Sam earn? (*Circle the correct letter.*)

A. 40%   **B.** 50%   **C.** 60%   **D.** 70%

2. Mrs. Long took her 20 students to recess. Eight of her students are on the slide and the rest are playing kickball. What percent of Mrs. Long's students are playing kickball? (*Show your work and circle your final answer.*)

1. Brent has an insect collection. Of the 20 insects in his collection, 6 are moths and the rest are butterflies. What percent of Brent's insect collection are butterflies? (*Show your work and circle your final answer.*)

2. Mrs. Chilek is giving her student, Rose, an opportunity to take a make-up test. After Rose completed the test and turned it in, Mrs. Chilek graded it. Mrs. Chilek found that Rose got 80% of the questions correct. What fraction of the questions did Rose get correct? (*Circle the correct letter.*)

A. $\frac{2}{3}$ **B.** $\frac{1}{2}$ **C.** $\frac{3}{4}$ **D.** $\frac{4}{5}$

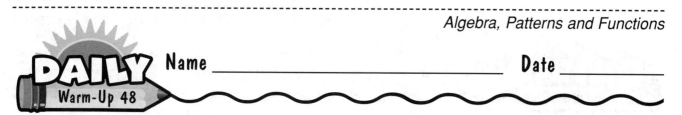

1. John has a lot of marbles. He has 3 green marbles for every 8 blue marbles. John has a total of 21 green marbles. How many blue marbles does John have? (*Show your work and circle your final answer.*)

2. For the sixth-grade field trip, 2 out of every 5 students want to go skating. There are 150 students in 6th grade. How many students in sixth grade prefer **not** to go skating? (*Show your work and circle your final answer.*)

Name _____ Date _____

Warm-Up 49

1. Solve the problems below. (*Show your work and circle your final answers.*)

   A. 96 x *y* = 3,360

   B. 78 x *y* = 4,368

2. Jimmy collects stamps. Over the summer, he collected 869 stamps. He added his new stamps to his collection of 6,750 stamps he already had. Of the 6,750 stamps, his father gave him 1,790 stamps when he was a boy. Which expression shows *x*, the number of stamps Jimmy collected on his own? (*Circle the correct letter.*)

   A. 6,750 – (2,200 + 869) = *x*

   B. 1,790 – (6,750 + 869) = *x*

   C. 869 + (6,750 + 1,790) = *x*

   D. (6750 + 869) – 1,790 = *x*

Name _____ Date _____

Warm-Up 50

1. Sergio is the lead pitcher on the baseball team. During the Friday night game, Sergio struck out 5 of every 15 batters. Which ratio compares the number of times Sergio struck a batter out to the number of times he did **not** strike a batter out? (*Show your work and circle your final answer.*)

2. Angela and Ed earned money from their parents by raking the lawn. Since Angela did other jobs around the house, she earned four times as much money as Ed earned. If Ed earned *n* dollars, which expression will show how much money Angela earned? (*Circle the correct letter.*)

   A. *n* ÷ 4   **B.** *n* – 4   **C.** 4 + *n*   **D.** 4*n*

Name _____ Date _____

1. Gordon's pet Boxer had 14 puppies. Two of the puppies were white and the rest were black, tan, or a combination of both. What ratio represents the number of white puppies compared to the total number of puppies Gordon's Boxer had? (*Show your work and circle your final answer.*)

2. Which rule goes with the table? (*Circle the correct letter.*)

A. $y - 5 = w$ **C.** $w \times 2 = y$

B. $y \times 5 = w$ **D.** $w \times 5 = y$

w	y
2	10
3	15
4	20
5	25

- -

Name _____ Date _____

1. Wanda has 4 jars of buttons. Altogether, she has 4,938 buttons. She has 1,594 buttons in the first jar, 1,250 buttons in the second jar, and 845 buttons in the third jar. How many buttons does Wanda have in the fourth jar? (*Show your work and circle your final answer.*)

2. Which two shapes will come next in the pattern? (*Circle the correct letter.*)

       _____ _____

A.    **B.**   **C.**   **D.**

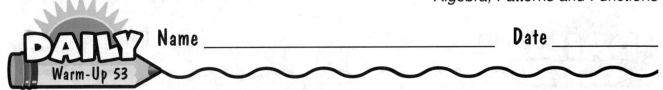

Name _____ **Date** _____

Warm-Up 53

1. Marcus and Mary built a house out of wooden cubes. Of the cubes, 0.35 were tan. The rest of the wooden cubes were black. What fraction (in lowest terms) of the cubes were black? (*Show your work and circle your final answer.*)

2. Freddy emptied his piggy bank. There were 580 coins inside the bank. Sixty-nine coins were dimes, 83 coins were nickels, 72 coins were quarters, 68 coins were fifty-cent pieces, 110 coins were silver dollars, and the rest of the coins were pennies. How many of the coins were pennies? (*Show your work and circle your final answer.*)

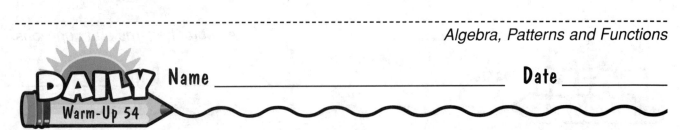

Name _____ **Date** _____

Warm-Up 54

1. Robin bought 3 books for $18 each, a new shirt for $38.50, and a new vacuum cleaner. Altogether, tax came to $68.78. Robin wrote a check for $210.78. How much did the vacuum cleaner cost (before tax)? (*Show your work and circle your final answer.*)

2. Mrs. Murphy bought a package of 800 sheets of construction paper. She is doing an art project with her students where each of her 35 students will need exactly 18 sheets. She plans to do the art project herself so she will have something to show the students as an example before they start. How many sheets of construction paper will Mrs. Murphy have left after the class completes the project? (*Show your work and circle your final answer.*)

Name _____ Date _____

1. Scott bought 6 boxes of chocolate candy for his store. There were 36 pieces of chocolate in each box. During the month, customers purchased all but 9 pieces. If p represents the number of chocolate candy pieces, which equation can be used to show the number of chocolate candy pieces purchased by customers? (*Circle the correct letter.*)

A. $(36 \times 6) + 9 = p$ **C.** $(36 + 6) - 9 = p$

B. $(36 \div 6) - 9 = p$ **D.** $(36 \times 6) - 9 = p$

2. Mike has a new fishing box the holds 18 fishing lures. Of the lures, 9 are orange. The rest are yellow and black. What is the ratio of orange fishing lures to yellow and black fishing lures? (*Show your work and circle your final answer.*)

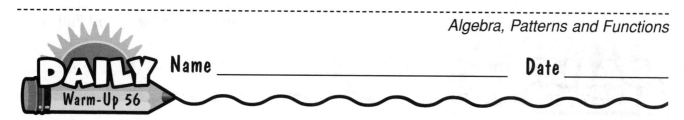

Name _____ Date _____

1. Warren has a photo album of his son's first birthday party. There are 30 pages in the photo album. The first 10 pages hold 8 pictures each. The remaining pages hold 10 pictures each. Which equation will find P, the total number of pictures the album can hold? (*Circle the correct letter.*)

A. $P = (30 \times 8) + (10 \times 10)$ **C.** $P = (8 \times 10) + (10 \times 30)$

B. $P = (10 \times 8) + (20 \times 10)$ **D.** $P = (8 \times 8) + (20 \times 30)$

2. Solve the equation below if $y = 4$ and $z = 5$. (*Show your work and write your final answer in the box.*)

$$y \times 12 - z = \boxed{}$$

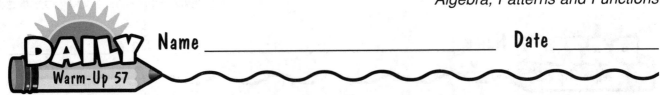

Name _____ **Date** _____

Warm-Up 57

1. Dana mailed graduation invitations to family and friends. She added a graduation picture in 2 out of every 6 invitations. Dana mailed a total of 180 invitations. Which statement about the number of graduation pictures Dana mailed is true? (*Circle the correct letter.*)

   A. Dana mailed a total of 120 graduation pictures.

   B. Dana mailed a total of 80 graduation pictures.

   C. Dana mailed a total of 60 graduation pictures.

   D. Dana mailed a total of 90 graduation pictures.

2. Terry gave 0.2 of the fish she caught to her mother and brother. What fraction shows the number of fish Terry gave her mother and brother? (*Show your work and circle your final answer.*)

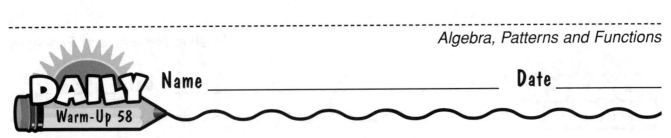

Name _____ **Date** _____

Warm-Up 58

1. Marybeth collects crystal bells. She keeps her collection on shelves in her living room. The first 3 shelves have 12 crystal bells each. The remaining 4 shelves have 9 crystal bells each. Write an equation that could be used to find *b*, the number of crystal bells on all shelves. (*Circle your final answer.*)

2. Of the 20 students in Mr. Matthew's math class, 12 wore blue shirts on Friday. What percent of the students in Mr. Matthew's class wore blue shirts on Friday? (*Show your work and circle your final answer.*)

Name _____ **Date** _____

1. Which rule goes with the table? (*Circle the correct letter.*)

A. $y^3 = x$ **C.** $x^3 = y$

B. $y^5 = x$ **D.** $x^5 = y$

x	y
2	8
4	64
6	216
8	512

2. Jeffrey is a great baseball player. During summer camp, he hit the ball out of the park 2 out of every 8 times he was at bat. What ratio compares the number of times Jeffrey hit the ball out of the park to the number of times he was at bat? (*Show your work and circle your final answer.*)

- -

Name _____ **Date** _____

1. In Mike's seashell collection, he has 18 small seashells and 54 large seashells. What fraction is equivalent to the ratio of the number of small seashells Mike has to the total number of shells in his collection? (*Show your work and circle your final answer.*)

2. Mrs. Branson ordered 36 markers for her students. Last week, she gave 3 students 2 markers each. This week, she gave 4 students 3 markers each. She then bought 2 packages with 12 markers in each package. Write an equation showing y, the number of pencils Mrs. Branson now has. (*Circle your final answer.*)

Name _____ **Date** _____

Warm-Up 61

1. Roy bought five 12-ounce colas for his grandchildren. He paid the cashier with a $10 bill. The cashier gave him $6.25 in change. Which equation below shows how to find *c*, the cost of one 12-ounce cola? (*Circle the correct letter.*)

A. ($10 – $6.25) ÷ 5 = *c*

C. ($10 – $6.25) ÷ 6 = *c*

B. ($12 – $10) ÷ 5 = *c*

D. ($10 + $6.25) ÷ 5 = *c*

2. Wanda is taking a bus to Arkansas to see her sister. On the bus, there are a total of 80 passengers. Thirty-two are males and the rest are females. What ratio compares the total number of males to the total number of females on the bus? (*Show your work and circle your final answer.*)

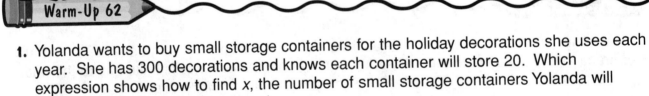

Name _____ **Date** _____

Warm-Up 62

1. Yolanda wants to buy small storage containers for the holiday decorations she uses each year. She has 300 decorations and knows each container will store 20. Which expression shows how to find *x*, the number of small storage containers Yolanda will need? (*Circle the correct answer.*)

A. 300 – 20 = *x*

C. 300 ÷ 20 = *x*

B. 300 + 20 = *x*

D. 300 x 20 = *x*

2. At the car wash, 2 out of every 3 vehicles washed were trucks. If there were a total of 36 vehicles washed yesterday morning, how many vehicles washed can be predicted to be trucks? (*Show your work and circle your final answer.*)

Answer Key

Warm-Up 1
1. 756 haircuts
2. B

Warm-Up 2
1. 4:3
2. $\frac{2}{3}$

Warm-Up 3
1. A. 2
   B. 32
2. C

Warm-Up 4
1. 377 pennies
2. 370 cans

Warm-Up 5
1. A. 105
   B. 133
   C. 115
   D. 307
2. $4\frac{3}{8}$ feet

Warm-Up 6
1. C
2. A. $y = 1\frac{1}{8}$
   B. $z = \frac{3}{4}$

Warm-Up 7
1. D
2. D

Warm-Up 8
1. 437 blue beads
2. Yes

Warm-Up 9
1. A
2. A

Warm-Up 10
1. 70%
2. A. 60%
   B. 76%

Warm-Up 11
1. B
2. 52 push mowers

Warm-Up 12
1. 3,772 roses
2. C

Warm-Up 13
1. A. $n = \frac{5}{12}$
   B. 5
2. B

Warm-Up 14
1. 78
2. D

Warm-Up 15
1. 22 customers
2. A

Warm-Up 16
1. C
2. 15 miles

Warm-Up 17
1. 12 points
2. 4

Warm-Up 18
1. $9.13
2. 0

Warm-Up 19
1. 82
2. 40, 48, 56

Warm-Up 20
1. D
2. 37

Warm-Up 21
1. 9
2. C

Warm-Up 22
1. D
2. range: 32
   mode: 12
   median: 16

Warm-Up 23
1. $50
2. C

Warm-Up 24
1. A
2. 5

Warm-Up 25
1. $\frac{2}{5}$
2. $\frac{5}{18}$

Warm-Up 26
1. Yes, the two ratios do form a proportion.
2. 18 baseball cards

Warm-Up 27
1. B
2. 468 cars

Warm-Up 28
1. 3,772 cherry snow cones
2. 54 puppies

Warm-Up 29
1. 24 eggs
2. 50 questions

Warm-Up 30
1. 40%
2. D

Warm-Up 31
1. B
2. 26 baskets

Warm-Up 32
1. 38
2. D

Warm-Up 33
1. B
2. $132 \div 11 = 12$
   $132 \div 12 = 11$
   $12 \times 11 = 132$
   $11 \times 12 = 132$

Warm-Up 34
1. C
2. 24,576 and 96

Warm-Up 35
1. B
2. D

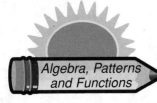

Answer Key

Warm-Up 36
1. C
2. A

Warm-Up 37
1. D
2. 24 cars

Warm-Up 38
1. 24 puppies
2. A

Warm-Up 39
1. $\dfrac{1}{12} = \dfrac{6}{72}$ or $\dfrac{12}{1} = \dfrac{72}{6}$
2. 35 red baseball caps

Warm-Up 40
1. 25 pages
2. 42, 48, 54

Warm-Up 41
1. 3:7
2. 7:3

Warm-Up 42
1. 48 basketballs
2. C

Warm-Up 43
1. A
2. C

Warm-Up 44
1. A
2. D

Warm-Up 45
1. A
2. B

Warm-Up 46
1. C
2. 60%

Warm-Up 47
1. 70%
2. D

Warm-Up 48
1. 56 blue marbles
2. 90 students

Warm-Up 49
1. A. $y = 35$
   B. $y = 56$
2. D

Warm-Up 50
1. 5:10 or 1:2
2. D

Warm-Up 51
1. $\dfrac{2}{14}$ or $\dfrac{1}{7}$
2. D

Warm-Up 52
1. 1,249 buttons
2. B

Warm-Up 53
1. $\dfrac{13}{20}$
2. 178 coins

Warm-Up 54
1. $49.50
2. 152 sheets

Warm-Up 55
1. D
2. 1:1

Warm-Up 56
1. B
2. 43

Warm-Up 57
1. C
2. $\dfrac{2}{10}$ or $\dfrac{1}{5}$

Warm-Up 58
1. $b = (3 \times 12) + (4 \times 9)$
2. 60%

Warm-Up 59
1. C
2. $\dfrac{1}{4}$

Warm-Up 60
1. $\dfrac{1}{4}$
2. $y = 36 - (3 \times 2) - (4 \times 3) + (2 \times 12)$

Warm-Up 61
1. A
2. 2:3

Warm-Up 62
1. C
2. 24 trucks